THE STORY OF THE DUBLIN INSTITUTE OF TECHNOLOGY

The Story of the Dublin Institute of Technology

Thomas Duff, Academic Registrar

Joseph Hegarty, Head, School of Culinary Arts
and Food Technology

Matthew Hussey, Director, Faculty of Science

BLACKHALL
Publishing

This book was typeset by
Gough Typesetting Services for
BLACKHALL PUBLISHING
26 Eustace Street
Dublin 2
Ireland

e-mail: blackhall@eircom.net
www.blackhallpublishing.com

ISBN 1 842180 13 4

A catalogue record for this book is
available from the British Library.

Printed in Ireland by
Colour Books

Dedication

This book is a tribute to:

- all the members of staff of the schools and colleges, for some forty years under the administration of the City of Dublin Technical Education Committee and the Rathmines Urban District Council Technical Instruction Committee, then for over sixty years under the aegis of the City of Dublin Vocational Education Committee, and latterly within the autonomous Dublin Institute of Technology
- the far-seeing members of those committees
- the administrative staff of those committees

who, down the years, worked often in adverse circumstances, to make the Dublin Institute of Technology the inspiring educational giant that it is today.

Acknowledgements

We are indebted to many people for their time and encouragement and in particular we would like to thank:

- Michael O'Donnell, former Principal of the College of Technology, Bolton Street, former Acting President and former Deputy President of the DIT, for inspiring this work through his deep commitment to the Institute

- Jimmie Robinson, for photographs, for help in finding sources and for the infection with the bug for investigating the past to illuminate the present and inspire the future

- Jim Cooke for access to sources about the earliest history of the system and for his painstaking and pioneering work in uncovering and writing about the proud history of the City of Dublin Vocational Education Committee and its predecessors

- Paddy Healy for his thorough review of an early draft and his constructive criticisms and comments

- Christine Hussey for her editorial review of the manuscript and for helping to improve the readability of the book

- Pat O'Neill, Tom Madden and Yvonne Farry for help in finding and confirming dates and other details

- CRH Ltd and Dublin Bus for financial support.

Thomas Duff
Joseph Hegarty
Matthew Hussey
May 2000

Contents

SECTION TWO: HIGHLIGHTS OF THE DIT'S ACADEMIC
PROFILE

SECTION THREE: A VIEW OF THE FUTURE OF THE DIT

Preface

This book traces the development of the Dublin Institute of Technology (DIT) from its origins over 113 years ago. There are many aspects of the history of the Institute and its predecessor colleges and schools that deserve study. There were many people who made significant contributions to its development and who deserve wider recognition, not only in the educational sphere but in the national arena as well. This book will be a great success if it stimulates such studies and related publications.

The aim of the book is to capture the broad sweep of the story of the DIT but not to describe the fine details of every development. In consequence some highlights, and indeed some weaknesses, do not receive the attention that they might deserve.

The book is directed primarily at the Institute community — academic and support staff, professional and industrial associates in Ireland and abroad, alumni and their families and students and their families. We hope it will add to their well founded pride in the Institute and its achievements. It is also directed at future students and their families and advisers in second level schools, to provide them with broad background information about the programmes, ethos and spirit of the Institute. The book will also be of interest to local and national politicians, as well as to local and national government officials, who have a major stake in the Institute and its progress. The book will further be of value as a reference to students of education at home and abroad as a perspective on the changing currents in the Irish educational system.

This book is offered as a record of achievement, in trust that the next generation will take the Institute to greater heights of educational service and accomplishment.

May 2000

Introduction

The Dublin Institute of Technology (DIT) was established by statute as an autonomous institution on 1 January 1993, under the Dublin Institute of Technology Act 1992, "to provide vocational and technical education and training for the economic, technological, scientific, commercial, industrial, social and cultural development of the state". It was constituted from the six higher education colleges of the City of Dublin Vocational Education Committee (CDVEC). These colleges, located in the city centre both south and north of the River Liffey, had provided applied and higher vocational education and training programmes, mainly in areas of technology and business, for over a century.

The six colleges that amalgamated to form the DIT, with the foundation year of each given in brackets, were as follows:

- College of Technology, Kevin Street, Dublin 8 (1887)
- College of Music, Chatham Row and Adelaide Road, Dublin 2 (1890)
- College of Commerce, Rathmines, Dublin 6 (1901)
- College of Marketing and Design, Mountjoy Square, Dublin 1 (formerly on Parnell Square, Dublin 1) (1905)
- College of Technology, Bolton Street, Dublin 1 (1911)
- College of Catering, Cathal Brugha Street, Dublin 1 (1941).

Since the earliest years the colleges developed programmes in different areas of speciality, with the underlying vision of providing the educational services needed by society — by students, industry, business, the community and particularly the disadvantaged sections of the population. The colleges responded flexibly and imaginatively to the changing needs arising from changes in technology in the city and in the country as a whole. In their new form as the DIT they continue to respond to the new challenges including those posed by the revolution in information technology and communications.

In the early years most of the programmes were at second level, but over the century, the Dublin colleges came to specialise mainly in higher level educational work, while second level work was transferred to other schools in the CDVEC system. At the present time the Institute offers close to 300 courses in a wide range of disciplines, in a multi-level context.

The colleges have grown and developed such that the annual enrolments are now about 22,000 — 10,500 full-time third level students, 4,000 apprentices and some 7,500 part-time, usually evening, students. The Institute has the highest student enrolment of all the higher education institutions in the state.

This book describes the main features of the evolution of the Institute, from its beginnings more than a century ago to its academic development over the past thirty years. The approach is firstly to provide a general historical chronology together with the macro-political factors influencing developments, then to review the highlights of the academic profile of the Institute and finally to consider the challenges facing it in the early years of the twenty-first century.

The growth of the colleges from which the DIT has been formed is traced from their origins in the Technical School established on Kevin Street in 1887. To provide the backdrop and context for this story, the highlights in the development of higher education in general and the other higher education institutions are also outlined.

The detailed review presented in this book describes the ways in which the DIT and its predecessor colleges, under the CDVEC and the earlier City of Dublin Technical Education Committee, contributed and continue to contribute to educating young people in Ireland and to developing Irish society, industry and higher education. While the Institute has withstood challenges and availed of many opportunities to improve the educational service it provides to the community, it will be apparent that it also missed valuable opportunities. The various judgements and evaluations made in this book at different junctures about the development of the Institute and its predecessor colleges clearly have the benefit of hindsight and should be taken in that light. They should also be taken in the context of the predominantly progressive and constructive thrust of the programmes developed across all the colleges.

The Institute and its predecessors pioneered applied education and training in a wide range of occupations, trades and skills, in close consultation with the relevant industries, professions and trade unions. Throughout their history they developed solutions in a wide range of disciplines to the complex and conflicting demands made on them by the short-term training needs of industry and business and the long-term educational needs of students. In this conflict, expressed in recent times as between, on one side, a possibly narrow instrumentalism or vocationalism focussing on instruction/training for the job, and on the other side, the broader educational development of the students for life, they strove to keep the interests of students at their core.

The Dublin colleges pioneered full-time education and practical training in applied areas that were not widely available due to the lack of a strong industrial infrastructure in the city and country. They helped to develop a range of new professions and the advanced training needed to establish and maintain them. They pioneered the development of technician and technologist training and education, a factor that helped in no small way to energise the emergence of Irish industry over the past thirty years. In that period the Institute has produced some 50,000 diploma, certificate and apprentice certificate graduates. It also developed an unprecedented partnership with the University of Dublin that has provided thousands of places on degree and professional courses during the rapid expansion in higher education that began in the 1970s and continued through the 1980s and 1990s. It has produced over 12,000 such graduates over the past twenty-five years. The DIT has provided, and continues to provide, access at all levels from apprentice to postgraduate level, with part-time, evening and full-time courses with clearly signposted transfer tracks between the different levels in most disciplines. Historically, in each academic year, it has provided more part-time and second-chance educational opportunities than all the other higher education institutions in Ireland combined. It pioneered applied research with strong industrial applicability at postgraduate level and recognised, at a very early stage, the key role of research and the related advancement of knowledge in underpinning all areas of higher education. It has maintained extensive and fruitful links with the professions, industry and business, nationally and internationally, for over a century.

As a multi-level higher education institution, the DIT continues this tradition and is developing and adapting it for future generations of students.

Historical Chronology of the Dublin Institute of Technology

CHAPTER 1

Technical Education in Ireland before 1922

This chapter gives an outline of the developments of the technical/vocational education system in the Dublin area from which the Dublin Institute of Technology (DIT) emerged.

EARLY TECHNICAL/VOCATIONAL EDUCATION

There was little coherent technical/vocational education in Ireland before the end of the 19th century. The Dublin Metropolitan School of Art had been established by the Royal Dublin Society in 1749. In 1849 a school of design had been set up in the premises of the Royal Cork Institution. Then in 1855 a school of art was set up in the premises of the Athenaeum Society of Limerick. Mechanics Institutes for the training of artisans were founded in a number of areas beginning in Dublin in 1837 and including one in Clonmel, Co. Tipperary which was established with the support of Thomas Bianconi in 1845.

After 1859, students in Ireland studied for examinations provided in science and art subjects by the Kensington Science and Art Department in London and teachers received payment-by-results. After the founding of the Royal College of Science in 1867 pressure developed in Ireland for a separate Irish science and art department to better serve industrial development in Ireland. The establishment of the City and Guilds of London Institute in 1880 provided examinations and payment-by-results for teachers, in more technical areas than the older science and art department scheme.

ORIGINS OF THE DUBLIN INSTITUTE OF TECHNOLOGY

The origins of Dublin Institute of Technology can be traced to the Irish Artisans' Exhibition, which was held in 1885 in premises located on the site of the present National Concert Hall in Earlsfort Terrace.[1] The exhibi-

---

1. Gleeson, M M, *Development of Technical Education in Dublin*, (Dublin: Associa-

tion was organised through the Workingmen's Club in Christchurch Place and was supported by a representative range of artisan delegates from the bookbinders, bricklayers, carpenters and joiners, coopers, cork-cutters, goldsmiths and jewellers, horseshoers, letterpress printers, plasterers, silk-weavers and stonecutters. The purpose of the exhibition was to encourage industry, "not in the form of capital but in the form of handicrafts . . . to produce home industry" and to "encourage technical education".

This latter purpose had been given added impetus by the report of the Samuelson Commission on Technical Education, which had sat from 1881 to 1884 and which recommended that municipally aided technical schools, on the successful continental model, be established throughout the United Kingdom.

Technical school, Kevin Street

At the conclusion of the artisans' exhibition, it was suggested that the premises on Earlsfort Terrace might continue to be used to provide education for the working classes of the city. A broadly based committee was established to advance the proposal, with Michael Davitt as one of its principal champions on Dublin Corporation, and Arnold Graves as the main promoter. After extensive deliberations it decided that more suitable accommodation for a school of the type envisaged was to be found at 18 Lower Kevin Street, on a site where William Fry & Co., cabinet makers and manufacturers of coachmakers' wares, had previously had a factory and where the present DIT faculty of science is located.

Financed by public subscription and aided by a grant from Dublin Corporation, the Kevin Street Technical School opened for classes in October 1887, with W. Vickers-Dixon as principal, ten part-time teachers and seventy-eight students divided into fifteen classes studying twelve different subjects. By the end of that first year a total of 220 students had attended. All classes were held in the evenings. There were three types of classes:

• science and art classes leading to examinations of the Science and Art Department, and for which payment-on-results was given

---

tion of Technical Education) 1956; de Lacy, H, *Vocational School to College of Technology, Jubilee Booklet,* (Dublin: City of Dublin Vocational Education Committee) 1980; Brennan, F M, Cooke, J, Mac Daeid, D A & Robinson, J, (Eds.), *Kevin Street College: One Hundred Years 1887-1987,* (Dublin: Dublin Institute of Technology/City of Dublin Vocational Education Committee) 1987; Duff, T J, *The Dublin Institute of Technology: A Study in Evolution,* MLitt Thesis, (Dublin: University of Dublin), 1995.

- technical classes leading to examinations of the City and Guilds of London Institute, for which payment-on-results was also given
- classes which led to school examinations.

The subjects taught in the 1888/1889 academic year were the following: practical plane and solid geometry, mathematics, theoretical and applied mechanics, machine construction and drawing, building construction and drawing, metal plate work, plumbing, carpentry and joinery, freehand drawing, modelling, theoretical and practical chemistry, sound, light and heat, electricity and magnetism, steam, photography, cookery, dressmaking and shorthand.

From its inception the school's management committee had representation from Dublin Corporation, a number of the trades and academics from the Royal College of Science and Trinity College Dublin.

Two years later, the Agriculture and Technical Instruction Act 1889 enabled local authorities to make a levy on the local rates (taxes) to support technical education and supplement the central government funding. The levy was limited to 1d per £1 valuation. This dual source of funding remained a feature of the Irish technical education system but the local rates contribution gradually lost its relative significance.

The additional funds available facilitated the development of technical and technological education in Dublin. The success of the Kevin Street school further encouraged this. As early as 1891, Arnold Graves advocated the need for two further schools, one on the north side of the Liffey and one at Ringsend to cater for fishery and navigation. The Pembroke Technical and Fishery Schools opened in Ringsend in 1893 under the aegis of the Pembroke Urban District Council. In the same year Dublin Corporation first implemented the Agriculture and Technical Education Act 1889 and with the additional funds provided additional classroom accommodation across the street from the Kevin Street school in 37 Lower Kevin Street.

By the academic year 1896/1897, the range of classes provided in the Technical School in Kevin Street, had multiplied. They attracted an enrolment of 925 and were offered in the following discipline areas:

- science (practical plane and solid geometry, machine construction and drawing, applied mechanics and steam, inorganic chemistry, organic chemistry, sound, light and heat, electricity and magnetism, mathematics, building construction)
- art (freehand, geometrical and model drawing, modelling in clay)
- technology (boot and shoemaking, carpentry and joinery, metal plate

work, plumbing, woodwork, building surveying, tailors' cutting, electric lighting, mechanical engineering, printers' and decorators' work)
* commerce (shorthand, book-keeping, writing, English, French, German, Irish)
* women's work (dressmaking, cookery and laundry work).

To help solve the problem of congestion in the school, an extension was started in 1899 and opened the following year. It provided an additional floor area of 1,500 m² to add to the 700 m² in the original building.

County councils and urban councils were set up throughout Ireland by the Local Government (Ireland) Act 1898. Then the Department of Agriculture and Technical Education (Ireland) Act 1899 extended the provisions of the United Kingdom 1889 Act throughout Ireland. This Act eventually led, in 1900, to the establishment in Ireland of the Department of Agriculture and Technical Instruction (DATI), which was to provide funds to promote technical education in different parts of the country. The Technical Education Committee (TEC) was formed in 1900 by Dublin Corporation to manage and govern technical education in the city. Forty-nine such local technical education committees were organised around the country to provide courses in art, technology and science in urban areas and in manual instruction, rural industries and domestic science in rural areas.

The enrolment in the Kevin Street school in 1900 had grown to 998, putting pressure on the available accommodation. The TEC leased 12 Rutland Square (Parnell Square after 1933) in 1904 and transferred the commercial classes there the following year. In 1906 the TEC made the decision to follow Arnold Graves' advice of 1891 to build a larger school on the north side of the city on Bolton Street. This was completed in 1911. At that stage classes in building construction and some engineering disciplines were transferred there.

Special courses in wireless telegraphy, telegraph construction and technical electricity for post office engineers were inaugurated in 1911 at the request of the Postmaster General. The wireless telegraphy course became controversial after 1916. The students on the course sought to have access to a practical ship's wireless set and the TEC attempted to acquire one, but permission was delayed by the Postmaster General in London, pending consideration by the naval and military authorities. Permission was eventually granted on condition that no external or internal aerial was erected, that no attempt would be made to communicate with other stations, and that the apparatus would be supervised by an officer of the post office. The apparatus would be unsealed by this officer at the start of a class and sealed again at its end, and each student of wireless telegraphy would have to be approved by the Postmaster General. Between January 1918 and March 1919, some 170 students entered this course and, of these, seven were not approved by the Postmaster General.

In the academic year 1912/1913, courses in chemistry for medical and pharmaceutical students, pharmacy, smiths' work, brass finishing, plasterer's work, painters' and decorators' work, tailors' cutting, woodcarving, clay modelling, stone and marble carving and decorative and ornamental ironwork, were taught in addition to those mentioned previously.

While the majority of the courses offered in the Kevin Street Technical School were at second level, i.e. for 14–16 year olds, there was a substantial element of higher level work as early as the first decade of this century. For instance in the academic year 1907/1908 students of the school won three of the five teacherships in training of the Royal College of Science, one taking the first place; four students qualified as teachers in chemistry under the DATI (Ireland); seven chemistry students were successful in the examinations for the Licentiateship of the Pharmaceutical Society of Ireland, one of them in first place; a number of students were successful in the degree examinations of the Royal University of Ireland, two achieving honours in chemistry; three students were successful in the external examinations of London University; the conjoint board of the Royal College of Physicians and the Royal College of Surgeons in Ireland inspected and recognised courses in physics and chemistry as satisfying the requirements for their first professional examinations. By 1910, students were asking that the Kevin Street college be made an examination centre for the London University BSc examinations, but this step was not taken until 1956.

From the foundation of the Kevin Street school there were elements of an academic structure. In 1896 for instance, there were five distinct categories of classes – science, art, technology, commercial and women's work. In 1911, after some courses had transferred to Chatham Row and Bolton Street, there were teachers employed in the following disciplines – mathematics, electrical engineering and physics, chemistry, botany, materia medica and pharmacy – which functioned as embryonic departments.

Municipal School of Music, Chatham Row

The Irish Artisans' Exhibition of 1885 also provided an impetus for the establishment of the School of Music. The Exhibition featured a competition for amateur bands organised by John O'Donnell.[2] Following a resolu-

---

2. Cooke, J, *A Musical Journey, 1890-1993, From Municipal School of Music to Dublin Institute of Technology*, (Dublin: Dublin Institute of Technology) 1994.

tion passed during the Exhibition, Mr. O'Donnell prepared a report on "The State of the National Bands of Ireland" in 1887. With support from the amateur bands in Dublin and the Royal Irish Academy of Music (RIAM), he subsequently persuaded Dublin Corporation to provide a grant of £300 for the establishment of the Municipal School of Music (MSM). This was housed in the Assembly Rooms, 58 South William Street (where the Civic Museum is now located) and opened in October 1890.

The Governors of the RIAM were to be the governing body of the MSM and initially they organised it as a complementary branch of the Academy. At its inception at least, teaching of singing, pianoforte, organ and stringed instruments was to be excluded, and the new school would concentrate on wind and percussion instruments. In its first year the new school provided classes in clarinet, cornet, drum, flute, oboe, piccolo, sax-horn and trombone for fifty-three students. In the following year alt horn, bombardon and euphonium were added to the instruments taught. How-ever by the third year, singing by the tonic solfa method was being taught to 36 students. In 1900, twenty-one students were studying the violin and the following year the violoncello had been added to the list.

In 1904 the TEC undertook a survey of technical education needs and concluded that the programmes of the MSM were too limited under the RIAM and could be extended and would flourish under the TEC. As a result, in that same year the TEC took over responsibility for the MSM from the Academy.

The inadequacies of the Assembly Rooms for the work of the MSM had been pointed out repeatedly. In 1907 the TEC transferred the music school to the newly acquired former fire station on Chatham Row, which it shared with the courses in printing until they were transferred to Bolton Street in 1911.

In the early decades of the school, all music teachers were employed on a part-time basis, depending on the demand for tuition in the relevant instruments. Nevertheless a measure of the success of the music school in those decades was the annual listing of its prizewinners in the Feis Ceoil, the Father Mathew Feis and the examinations of the London School of Music.

Municipal Technical Institute, Rathmines

The Rathmines Urban District Council (UDC) established the Rathmines Municipal Technical Institute at 24 Rathmines Road in 1901. This was administered by the Rathmines Technical Instruction Committee (TIC), a sub-committee of the UDC. The technical institute initially had a school of commerce only. In its first academic year it catered for 333 evening students, one third of them women. The declared aims of the institute were to work closely with commerce in developing courses for "persons of either sex", and "ultimately to include a complete provision for higher commercial education for both the population of the Urban District itself and the neighbouring City of Dublin".[3] In 1908 a school of domestic economy, housed in rented premises at 52A Carlton Terrace in Upper Rathmines, was established by the TIC.

General commercial and language courses as well as specialised courses for bank, railway and insurance clerks were provided. The courses for railway clerks were designed in consultation with the four Dublin railway companies. The bank clerks' courses were recognised by the Institute of Bankers in Ireland and were taught in part by bank officials. The courses for insurance clerks were developed in collaboration with the Chartered Insurance Institute and taught partly by officials of major insurance companies.

By 1912 there was a total enrolment of 509 students, 333 men and 176 women.

In 1913, a new building accommodating the technical institute and the Rathmines Public Library was first occupied. This allowed the overall enrolment to rise from 927 (345 men and 582 women) in 1913 to 1620 (612 men and 1008 women) in 1925.[4] This new development brought together under one roof the schools of commerce and domestic economy. At this stage the higher commercial subjects taught included commerce, accountancy, accountants' arithmetic, commercial geography, commercial history, auditing, commercial law, government accounting and finance, banking practice, law of banking, economics, statistical methods, foreign exchange, language and insurance. The courses in the school of domestic economy tended to be at junior or second level.

Technical School, Rutland Square

In 1905 12 Rutland (later Parnell) Square was acquired by the TEC and 18 Rutland Square was acquired in 1912. This latter site became for some 50 years a centre for commercial education and the teaching of domestic economy, mainly at the second level. Courses offered in the early years included book-keeping, accountancy, business methods, economics, com-

3. *Formal Opening of Phase 1, DIT Aungier Street*, (Dublin: Dublin Institute of Technology) 1996.
4. Clampett, G J T, *Summary of Evidence Submitted to the Commission of Enquiry into Technical Education*, (Dublin: Rathmines Technical Instruction Committee) 1926.

mercial correspondence, commercial arithmetic, commercial geography, shorthand, typewriting and retail grocery. Over the following years courses in Irish, French, German, health and life insurance, actuarial work and commercial law were added.

In 1915 the school of commerce in the Rutland Square school introduced a scheme to draw employers into the technical education system so as to provide a wider range of employment opportunities to students. With the involvement of employers in course design and work placement, day courses, initially for boys but later in the 1920s for girls as well, were developed·in business methods and in shirt and clothing manufacture.

Technical Institute, Bolton Street

In 1906 the TEC was given approval by the DATI (Ireland) for the building of a new technical institute at Bolton Street on the site of the old European Hotel.[5] The plans were ready in 1908 for what was to be the first building in the country specifically designed and built for technical and technological education. Completed in 1911, the building was opened for classes in the autumn of that year. Courses in construction and civil and mechanical engineering, which had already been developed in Kevin Street, were transferred to that site. A new course in building construction for architectural students was inaugurated at the request of the Architectural Association of Ireland. Courses in aeroplane construction were introduced in that first academic year, the year that Bleriot first flew a heavier-than-air machine across the English Channel. A course in land surveying was initiated and plans made for a course in motor engineering. The printing courses that had already transferred in 1907 from Kevin Street to Chatham Row, transferred to the Bolton Street institute in 1911. Indeed in the initial years the only full-time staff members in the Bolton Street Technical Institute were in the printing area, which in 1914 developed the first day-release apprenticeship courses in the country, three afternoons each week, for compositor and letterpress machine operators.

Most classes in the early years were held in the evenings. In 1920 however, additional full-time staff, including two joint principals, were appointed and the first full-time courses were begun that same year under a day apprentice scholarship scheme. The TEC awarded scholarships to

---

5.   O'Dwyer, D, *College of Technology, Bolton Street, Jubilee Booklet,* (Dublin: City of Dublin Vocational Education Committee) 1980; O'Dwyer, D & O'Donnell, M, *A Short Historical Profile, Souvenir Booklet to Commemorate the Official Opening of the Extension to the College of Technology, Bolton Street*, (Dublin: City of Dublin Vocational Education Committee) 1989.

selected students for a two-year full-time course in a trade and these two years counted as the first years of the student's apprenticeship. These day junior technical courses began in 1922 and continued until 1958, when they were transferred to second-level schools within the CDVEC system.

OTHER HIGHER EDUCATION INSTITUTIONS IN IRELAND

Before independence the main institutions of higher education in Ireland were the universities. The foundation dates of the university-level institutions in Ireland before 1922[6] together with their current enrolments, are provided in table 1.1. The establishment of Saorstát Éireann (Irish Free State) in the twenty-six counties and the state of Northern Ireland in the six counties in 1922, divided the administration of education in Ireland, including higher education into the two jurisdictions.

Table 1.1 University-level institutions in Ireland before 1922, with the year of foundation and equivalent full-time student enrolment in 1999/2000

Institution	Year of foundation	Current enrolment
University of Dublin (Trinity College Dublin, TCD)	1591	13,700
Royal College of Surgeons in Ireland	1784	
St. Patrick's College, Maynooth	1795	
National University of Ireland, Maynooth, NUI Maynooth		4,700
Queen's University, Queen's Colleges	1845	
Catholic University	1851	
Royal College of Science	1867	
Royal University of Ireland	1879	
National University of Ireland (NUI)	1908	
University College Cork, UCC, now NUI Cork		11,300
University College Dublin, UCD, now NUI Dublin		17,700
University College Galway, UCG, now NUI Galway		9,900

---

6. McElligott, T J, *Education in Ireland,* (Dublin: Institute of Public Administration) 1966; Coolahan, J, *Irish Education: History and Structure,* (Dublin: Institute of Public Administration) 1981.

Summary

From their very beginnings, the colleges that now constitute the DIT offered education and training at the leading edge of technology. They sought
to determine the needs of industry, business and commerce in Dublin and
nationally, and developed educational and training courses in disciplines
and areas not catered for by the rest of the educational system. The courses
offered had a strong vocational and applied thrust underpinned by a sound
knowledge base. They provided educational opportunities for women from
the early days and took measures to deliver educational opportunities to
the less privileged in society and the broad layers of working people.

These characteristics were to shape the policies and commitments of
the colleges that have become the DIT.

Chapter 2

Development of the Dublin Colleges to the Dublin Institute of Technology

The City of Dublin Vocational Education Committee (CDVEC) was established under the Vocational Education Act 1930. With Louis Ely O'Carroll as Chief Executive Officer, the CDVEC became responsible after 1930 for the existing technical institutes in Dublin located at Kevin Street, Chatham Row and Bolton Street, and other technical schools including that at Rutland/Parnell Square. In relation to the city of Dublin, the benefits of the Act were strengthened by the passing of the Greater Dublin Act 1930, which brought the urban districts of Pembroke and Rathmines into the city administrative area. In particular this brought the Rathmines Technical Institute and the Pembroke Technical and Fishery School at Ringsend into the CDVEC in 1932.

The list below shows the Chief Executive Officers (CEO) of the CDVEC from 1930 to the present day.

Chief Executive Officers of the CDVEC	
Louis Ely O'Carroll	1930–1943
Henry Thunder (Acting)	1943–1944
Martin Gleeson	1944–1970
Jeremiah Sheehan	1970–1973
Hugh Healy (Acting)	1973–1975
Jeremiah Sheehan	1975–1978
John McKay (Acting)	1978–1980
Liam Arundel	1980–present day

DEVELOPMENTS IN THE DUBLIN COLLEGES UNDER THE VOCATIONAL EDUCATION ACT

In the early 1930s the CDVEC established a board of studies comprising its CEO and the principals of the five technical institutes/schools, to advise it on educational matters relating to them. Over the years the board of studies provided academic and organisational oversight and cohesion. It served essentially as an embryonic academic council for the institutes/colleges and the foundation of the developments that led eventually to the Dublin Institute of Technology (DIT) can be discerned in its work.

In 1936 a committee of the board of studies formulated an ambitious strategic restructuring plan for the development of the technical education system in the Dublin area. This plan envisaged five specialised technical institutes in the central city zone and a number of less specialised regional schools. The five technical institutes were to be designated:

• the College of Technology — a new building, centrally located, to replace that at Kevin Street

• the High School of Commerce — a new building, centrally located, to accommodate the programmes provided in the building at Rathmines

• the School of Trades and Crafts — Bolton Street

• the School of Domestic Science — a new building to be built on a site at Cathal Brugha Street

• the School of Music — in new premises to replace the building at Chatham Row.[1]

A possible departmental structure of each of these colleges was outlined, together with how it might evolve over time. The colleges were to be authorised to grant diplomas in respect of approved courses of study. Recognition of these courses and qualifications by the relevant professional bodies was to be obtained through the design of the courses and the alignment of their syllabuses to the educational requirements of those bodies. Courses would be provided on a full-time basis by day and on a part-time basis in the evenings. The colleges would provide for the training of teachers in science and technology. In addition, they would offer refresher courses to help keep teachers in touch with the most recent developments in these disciplines. A significant element of the plan was that each college would also provide facilities for research in collaboration with industry.

Not all the strands of this restructuring plan came to fruition as circumstances changed and World War II intervened. Nevertheless, many aspects were implemented in some form over time as resources and government priorities allowed. Furthermore, the plan served to inform the

---

1. *Organisation and Development of the Scheme of Technical Education, Interim Report of the Board of Studies Committee* (Dublin: City of Dublin Vocational Education Committee), 1936.

general ambition of the CDVEC and the staff of the colleges for the next half-century.

The colleges also had a considerable commitment to providing education for 14–16 year-old students. This second level work was gradually devolved to new second-level schools within the CDVEC system but continued in the Rathmines college until 1980. It continues in the College of Music to this day.

In the twenty years from 1934 to 1954 the total enrolment each year in the CDVEC system rose from 12,830 to 23,169, while the number of annual teaching hours increased from 109,000 to 338,000.

Teaching staff

Throughout the history of the Dublin colleges there has been heavy reliance on part-time teachers in all of the colleges — a factor that did not promote academic cohesion or long-term planning. Nevertheless, the importance of teachers in bringing about change in the colleges is fundamental. They continue to be strategic participants in the evolution of the DIT. Their capacities to function as designers, producers and transmitters of knowledge and skills remain the cornerstone of the vitality of the DIT. Until the early 1950s, most full-time teaching staff members were on the basic grade of Class III teacher. This grade had a common standard salary scale, applicable to all primary and post-primary teachers. In the aftermath of World War II it proved difficult to retain part-time teachers in engineering, science and business. In order to solve staffing problems, the higher technological/commercial lecturer grade was developed. The minimum requirements for recruitment to this lecturer grade were an honours degree or equivalent in a relevant discipline together with at least three years' experience in industry. Significantly, until the introduction of the new grade of assistant lecturer in 1999, these continued to be the minimum requirements for recruitment to lecturing staff in the colleges for over 50 years.

This new lecturer grade was to be a key development that facilitated the emergence of higher level programmes in the Dublin colleges. Indeed, such lecturer grades were generally available only to teachers engaged mainly in professional and advanced technician diploma courses. Thus the expansion of higher level programmes led to the increase in the number of teaching staff with specialist background and skills at lecturer grade. In turn this enabled the design and delivery of further higher level programmes.

Changes in titles of colleges

At the end of the 1950s, in recognition of the changing nature of the work of the colleges, but also in broad pursuance of the different elements of the 1936 strategic plan, the CDVEC decided to rename each of the six higher education technical institutes/schools/colleges as a college. Each was assigned a principal and a departmental or school structure broadly based on academic disciplines. The existing institutes were renamed as follows:

• the Kevin Street Institute of Science and Technology became the College of Technology, Kevin Street

• the Municipal School of Music became the College of Music, Chatham Row

• Rathmines Technical Institute became the College of Commerce, Rathmines

• Parnell Square School of Commerce and Retail Distribution became the College of Marketing and Design, Parnell Square

• Bolton Street Technical Institute became the College of Technology, Bolton Street

• St Mary's College of Domestic Science became the College of Catering, Cathal Brugha Street.

This organisational structure continued until the proposed faculty structure reorganisation in the statutorily established DIT in the late 1990s (see Chapter 6).

In 1963, the CDVEC decided to establish six separate college councils as a move to create an academic and administrative structure for the colleges. These councils consisted of nominees of the CDVEC, the local principal and local staff and student representatives. Their function was to oversee the management of each college. Two years later the CDVEC appointed a secretary/registrar to manage the administrative and other non-academic staff in each college, and to oversee such matters as the registration of students, student records, accounts and finances, examinations and building maintenance.

REVIEW OF DEVELOPMENTS IN THE INDIVIDUAL COLLEGES

Institute of Science and Technology/College of Technology, Kevin Street

In 1931, after the implementation of the Vocational Education Act, a course for 'kinema' operators was initiated, as well as a two-year electrical engineering course for trainees in the electrical trades at the Kevin Street Institute of Science and Technology. An electrical apprentice course was begun in 1938 at the request of the Electricity Supply Board.

The Dublin Branch of the Irish Bakers', Confectioners' and Allied Workers' Amalgamated Union established the Dublin School of Bakery in 1935 and in 1937 agreed with the CDVEC to transfer it to the Kevin Street college. Up to that time the bakery trade did not have an organised training scheme and no moves were made initially to develop a bakery apprenticeship system under the Apprenticeship Act 1931. The first classes for bakery apprentices were offered in 1938 and, after a short period, these came to be accepted as the formal educational element of a new bakery apprenticeship scheme. By prescribing the requirements for entry and setting out education and training syllabuses, these courses helped to lay the foundation for the bakery trade in Ireland.

When World War II broke out, demand for higher level courses increased considerably. New courses in radio service work and applied science and mathematics began in 1940. The latter course developed into a pre-university course, which prepared students for the matriculation examinations of the National University of Ireland. A three-year full-time course in radio engineering was established in 1942. At the same time, one-year full-time courses in science for opticians, pharmacists and radiographers were also offered. An aircraft radio officers' course also began in the early 1940s.

Meanwhile, courses leading to the external BSc examinations of London University in electrical engineering, physics and chemistry, offered since the early years of the century, continued to be popular. In the same period courses in arts and related crafts as well as in aspects of industrial chemistry — gas manufacture, oils and fats, fuel technology — declined and eventually ceased, while courses in welding transferred to Bolton Street.

With the development of full-time courses a range of what are now known as academic quality assurance issues needed to be addressed, such as structured syllabuses, subject and discipline experts as teachers, clear schemes of instruction, well defined academic prerequisites and certain standards of mathematics and physics. In the early post-war years, the new higher technological lecturer grade helped to ensure that a community of teachers, suitably educated and trained, was available.

In 1947 there were three departments in the Kevin Street college — pure and applied science, electrical engineering technology and telecommunications engineering. By 1950 there were twenty-two full-time staff in these departments. They catered for some 2,000 students in total, most of them attending evening courses, but including about 350 full-time and 200 part-time day students. The building was fully occupied and frequently overcrowded.

By the mid-1950s the Kevin Street college, then known as the Institute of Science and Technology, provided courses in science, electrical, radio and telecommunications engineering, radio servicing, cinema, bakery and boot-making trades, marine radar and air navigation and science courses for ophthalmic opticians, health inspectors and marine radio officers. It also had a junior technical school. During the 1950s courses containing a wider range of subjects were developed. The radio engineering and chemistry courses included mathematics and physics. Other new courses initiated during the 1950s were a health inspectors' diploma, a senior science course for the English GCE 'O' and 'A' level examinations, a science laboratory technicians' course, a post-office technicians' course and, in 1959, a three-year ophthalmic and dispensing opticians' course. Evening courses tended to require attendance on three evenings each week. Target objectives, such as specified examinations, were established for each course and rules for progression into later years of the course set out. Given the limited teaching and accommodation resources, some older courses had to be discontinued. These included pharmacy, pharmaceutical chemistry, milk processing and brewing programmes.

By the end of the 1950s the Institute of Science and Technology had been redesignated a College of Technology by the parent CDVEC. By then, full-time day courses constituted the main thrust of the programmes in the college.

Efforts to relieve the overcrowding in the college included the acquisition of neighbouring sites, about 0.8 hectare in total, extending back from Kevin Street to Camden Row. In 1953 the Department of Education agreed to a major building programme to accommodate the departments of pure and applied science, electrical engineering, electrical installation work and telecommunications engineering, which were then flourishing in the college. After an extensive planning exercise, construction commenced in 1963. The new college building was completed in 1968 and provided about 14,000 square metres of new accommodation, including some 6,500 square metres of highly specialised laboratories for the engineering and science disciplines in the Kevin Street college.

Principals of the Kevin Street college	
W. Vickers-Dixon	1887–1901
Louis Ely O'Carroll	1901–1931
Edward Morton	1932–1952
Martin Cranley	1952–1962
Hugh de Lacy	1962–1982
Frank Brennan	1982–1993

Through consultation with the relevant professional bodies and the college advisory committees, the Kevin Street college started a number of post-leaving certificate technician courses during the 1960s, which evolved from earlier part-time courses. In 1960 an electrical engineering technician course started. Two years later a telecommunications and electronics technician course was initiated. An evening course in medical laboratory technology began in 1963 and this was replaced by a full-time course in 1965. In 1967 a part-time course in professional photography was started and, in 1969, a full-time technician diploma course in applied science, later with options in biology, chemistry and physics. A technician certificate course in applied science began in 1970.

In 1965 an apprenticeship course for dental technicians began and the Kevin Street college was designated as an approved centre. During this decade also a number of second-level courses were transferred from the college to other CDVEC schools. Thus the pre-university course moved to the Ringsend Technical Institute (formerly the Pembroke Technical and Fishery School) and the senior science course was distributed among a number of other second-level schools.

Until 1968 most of the courses prepared students for external examinations of the City and Guilds of London Institute and of London University, among others. However, in 1966 the professional electrical engineering course was reorganised as an honours diploma course of the college and two external examiners from different universities were appointed as external peer reviewers. The graduates of the course were accepted by the professional institution for membership and by universities at home and abroad for postgraduate work. From the start, the course had the status of an honours university degree course.

In the latter part of the 1960s it was decided to introduce academic awards of the college for existing full-time and part-time courses. Thus were established the technician engineer and engineering technician diplomas, and the technician diploma in applied science. From the outset these were readily given recognition by the professional institutions in Ireland and internationally and by industry and state organisations.

In the midst of these rapid academic developments, the administrative organisation of the college was also reviewed. In 1963 the CDVEC agreed to expand the previous four departments to seven — mathematics, physics, chemistry with biology, telecommunications, electrical engineering, electrical trades and general studies. Each department had a head and assistant head, each at senior lecturer grades, who were responsible for managing the department and providing leadership in the discipline.

Degree courses under the partnership agreement (see Chapter 4) with the University of Dublin and other higher level courses were developed in the Kevin Street college during the 1970s, 1980s and 1990s (See Chapter 8). These courses were in:

• applied sciences — biology, biomedical sciences, chemistry, computer science, food science, human nutrition and dietetics, mathematics, medical laboratory sciences, physics, optometry, photography
• electrical and electronic engineering — electrical power, control systems, telecommunications, electrical/electronic drafting, electronics technology
• languages and business
• bakery production and management.

By the late 1990s, the Kevin Street college encompassed the following range of disciplines, many heavily dependent on laboratory services: biological sciences, chemistry, control and electrical engineering, electrical installation, communications and electronic engineering, languages and industrial studies, mathematics, statistics and computer studies and physics (including optometry).

Municipal School of Music/College of Music, Chatham Row

The overwhelming majority of the work in the Municipal School of Music (MSM) in the 1930s was in the area of part-time and continuation education. In relation to training in musical instruments, individual tuition was the mode of teaching and students were recruited at less than twelve years of age. At that time a system of internal assessment and diplomas indicating standards of attainment was introduced to replace the previous practice of relying on the examinations of external bodies. The accommodation available on Chatham Row was very limited for the numbers of students taking classes, and in the light of the need for large spaces for orchestral and choral training. Furthermore, there were no full-time teachers in the school and therefore coherent academic planning was very difficult. In the 1936 plan of the CDVEC to develop five technical institutes, new premises to replace those at Chatham Row and serve as the School of Music were envisaged. In the plan there would be day and evening classes in the theory and practice of music, singing and elocution and in the art of music teaching in six areas — instrumental instruction, band and orchestra, singing and voice culture, Irish music, music education and organ and choir.

During the years of World War II, a diploma course for music teachers was introduced, but the other ambitious reforms remained largely unfulfilled.

By the mid-1950s the Municipal School of Music on Chatham Row offered part-time diploma courses with theoretical and practical education/training in the following instruments and topics: pianoforte, violin, viola, violoncello, double bass, harp, organ, uileann pipes, percussion, wind instruments, singing and voice production, Gaelic singing, sight reading, elocution, music and aural training, harmony and chamber music. Enrolments were very high, having risen from 1,400 in 1947 to about 2,500 in 1957. Unlike the other colleges under the aegis of the CDVEC, the work of the Municipal School of Music was mostly at the junior (second and even primary) levels and involved part-time students.

Directors/Principals of the College of Music	
Arthur Warren Darley	1928–1929
John F. Larchet	1929–1931
Maud Davin	1931–1944
Joseph S. O'Brien	1944–1953
Michael McNamara	1953–1969
J. J. O'Reilly	1969–1972
Frank Heneghan	1973–1993

In 1962 the Department of Education raised the question of the possible co-ordination of the work of the College of Music and the Royal Irish Academy of Music (RIAM). Discussions revealed the differences in approach between the two institutions, the College of Music being oriented to musical education for the masses and the RIAM possibly having a more elite orientation. A similar proposal was made in the recommendations of the Commission on Higher Education in 1967. While it was not implemented, the proposal did plant the seed of the idea for a national conservatory of music, which is again in the public domain at the present time.

During the 1960s full-time staff numbers increased so that by the early 1970s there were eighteen full-time teachers providing instrumental teaching to some 1,700 students. A two-year professional diploma course for performers and teachers of music was also introduced.

The degree courses in music (music education, music performance) developed since 1985 under the partnership agreement with the University of Dublin are outlined in Chapter 8, as are the other higher level courses in music teaching and speech and drama developed in recent years.

Rathmines Technical Institute/College of Commerce, Rathmines

An extension to the Rathmines Technical Institute was built in 1944 which facilitated the enrolment of additional student numbers. Some time later the institute was renamed the High School of Commerce and in 1956 the CDVEC designated it the College of Commerce. At that stage there were two schools in the college — general studies and business studies. The majority of the enrolment was in full-time continuation education courses at the second level in the school of general studies. This school also prepared students for pre-university matriculation examinations.

In the late 1950s up to 2,500 students enrolled each year on higher level evening courses leading to the examinations of professional and other examining bodies in advertising, cost and works accountancy, government accountancy, auditing, company secretaryship, banking, economics, law, languages, foreign trade, management studies, sales management, inland and air transport, commercial and secretarial studies and domestic science.

Principals of the College of Commerce, Rathmines	
Charles Oldham	1901–1909
Arthur Williamson	1910–1919
George J. T. Clampett	1919–1950
Seán Ó Ceallaigh	1951–1973
Patrick Crowley (Acting)	1973–1975
John McKay	1975–1981
Vincent Farrington (Acting)	1978–1980
James Hickey	1981–1993

A third school — management studies — was added in 1958 and it specialised in part-time and short courses in co-operation with industry and commerce. These courses covered themes such as foremanship and supervision, management principles, interviewing techniques, office management, financial accounting, personnel management, effective speaking, work study and training within industry.

In the early 1960s the Rathmines college initiated the first four-year full-time degree level course in business outside the universities. Computer studies, as well as accountancy and economics, were emphasised from the start. Additional professional courses in marketing, sales management, personnel management, credit management, training management, work study, supervision, purchasing, public administration and hospital administration were initiated in co-operation with professional bodies.

About the same time the college developed full-time courses in journalism (two-year certificate course), advertising (one-year certificate course), public relations (one-year certificate course) and communications (three to four-year diploma course), reflecting and contributing to the birth of the media industry and, in particular, the electronic media industry in Ireland. The innovations were developed in close consultation and agreement with the industries and the relevant professional organisations.

During the 1960s the school of management studies, continuing to focus on short courses for industry and with the support of staff members in schools across the Dublin colleges, introduced new modules in areas such as communications, marketing and sales, production management, quality control, organisation and methods, transport, maintenance, electronics, engineering technology and industrial safety.

Degree courses in communications (film/broadcasting, journalism), business studies, management services and health services management were developed over the past twenty five years in the Rathmines college under the partnership agreement with the University of Dublin (see Chapter 4). Other higher level and postgraduate courses were developed in journalism, business information systems, international economics and human resource management, transport management and professional accountancy. (These developments are discussed in Chapter 8.)

School of Commerce and Retail Distribution/College of Marketing and Design, Parnell Square (later on Mountjoy Square)

The Parnell Square site provided space for the offices of the City of Dublin TEC and subsequently those of the CDVEC after its formation in 1930, and before the transfer of its offices to the former Town Hall of the Pembroke Urban District Council in Ballsbridge, in 1951.

In 1949 courses and training programmes for the retail distribution trades — grocery, drapery, victualling and hairdressing — were first introduced in the Parnell Square school. These courses were attended by apprentices on day release from their employment and led to apprentice certificate and diploma awards of the different chambers of trade. Advisory committees involving both employer organisations and trade unions supported the courses in the different trades. Language and art and design were offered as service courses to the main retail distribution and marketing courses. Since that time the school has occupied a unique and pioneering role as the only institution in Ireland specifically offering courses for all elements of the retail trades.

By 1956, the Parnell Square school was known as the School of Commerce and Retail Distribution and offered higher level courses in retail drapery, grocery and victualling trades, retail management, secretarial studies, languages and domestic science. It also had a junior (second-level) school offering continuation education courses in commercial subjects for boys and girls.

Principals of the College of Marketing and Design	
Martin R. Wheeler	1911–1919
J. C. MacGuigan	1919–1947
Pauline Beirne	1948–1977
Thomas Madden	1977–1992
Paul O'Sullivan (Acting)	1992–1993

By the end of the 1960s the higher level courses had been drawn into the ambit of the Academic Council and the title of the Parnell Square school had been changed to the College of Marketing and Design with three schools — design, marketing studies and distribution studies.

The school of distribution studies offered part-time day-release courses at trainee level in distribution management, bar management and basic management, as well as an extended range of apprentice courses in the bookselling/stationery, florist, grocery, hardware, meat, wholesale and retail drapery, public bar and hotel bar businesses.

The school of design had earlier been a service area for the distributive trades but developed into wider areas of design and later art. The school of marketing studies developed broadly from the same origins to offer courses leading to examinations of different professional bodies.

Higher level courses, initially offered on a part-time basis but gradually introduced on a full-time basis also, included those leading to professional certificates and diplomas in areas including visual communication, environmental design, interior design, exhibition design, set and stage design, shopfitting, display design, furniture design, graphics, marketing, distribution management and bar management, and training for proprietors of retail meat, drapery and bar establishments.

The degree courses in marketing techniques and marketing administration developed in the Parnell Square/Mountjoy Square college since 1976 under the partnership agreement with the University of Dublin (see Chapter 4), together with other higher level courses in art, environmental design, visual communication design, marketing, business studies and retailing, developed over the past thirty years, are outlined in Chapter 8.

Technical Institute/College of Technology, Bolton Street

Academic developments in the Bolton Street Technical Institute during the 1930s and 1940s closely paralleled those in the Kevin Street Institute of Science and Technology. They included the development and expansion of the day-release schemes for apprentice students from the engineering and construction industries and the fostering of strong links with industry through the mechanism of advisory committees. In the post-war period, the demand for technological expertise grew and higher level courses in the Bolton Street college expanded rapidly. These higher level full-time courses were generally designed to prepare students for the examinations of professional bodies such as architecture, quantity surveying and the engineering institutions related to the Bolton Street college disciplines.

In 1956 the technical institute in Bolton Street offered full-time courses in architecture, surveying, building trades, civil, mechanical, motorcar and aeronautical engineering, mechanical engineering trades and printing and book production, and woodwork teachers' training. At that time the college also had a substantial junior technical school, but elements of that work were gradually transferred to new second-level schools within the CDVEC system to allow accommodation for the growing volume of higher level work.

Directors/Principals of Bolton Street college	
John Ryan	1912–1919
Ernest E. Joynt (mechanical engineering)	1920–1942
William J. Davidson (architecture and building trades)	1920–1938
Martin Keady	1942–1952
Donal O'Dwyer	1952–1973
Jack Barry	1973–1980
Michael O'Donnell	1980–1993

In 1962 the Linen Hall building close to the Bolton Street college, formerly a linen mill destroyed by fire during the war of independence and rebuilt as a warehouse, was acquired by the CDVEC. The building was reconstructed and refurbished to accommodate courses in the construction trades and the School of Trades in the Linen Hall was opened in 1963.

These additional resources facilitated the establishment in the Bolton Street college, in the mid-1960s, of the first full-time technician courses in Ireland in architecture, construction and related engineering disciplines. These led to certificate and diploma awards of the Bolton Street college. The diploma awards soon came to be accepted by the relevant professional bodies as fully meeting their academic requirements for membership.

Since 1975 the Bolton Street college has developed a range of degree courses in engineering (mechanical, structural, manufacturing, building services), architecture, property economics and construction economics under the partnership agreement with the University of Dublin (see Chapter 4). These and other higher level courses in printing, architectural technology, construction technology, geo-surveying, auctioneering and estate agency, civil engineering, building services and motor industry management, developed over the past thirty years, are outlined in Chapter 8.

By the 1990s, the Bolton Street college catered for the following disciplines, most heavily dependent on laboratory and specialised studio resources: architecture and town planning, surveying and building, construction trades, engineering technology, transport engineering, science, mathematics and general studies, engineering trades and printing.

St Mary's College of Domestic Science/College of Catering, Cathal Brugha Street

A major element of the CDVEC's 1936 strategic plan was implemented when, in 1941, the first designated third-level college, St Mary's College of Domestic Science, was opened on Cathal Brugha Street to provide a three-year diploma course to train domestic science teachers, a range of one-year courses in household and institutional management and a one-year course for the training of apprentice chefs.[2] In addition, the school of domestic economy from the Rathmines Technical Institute and the school of domestic science from Parnell Square were transferred to Cathal Brugha

---

2. O'Connor, N (ed.), *Dublin College of Catering 1941–1991* (Dublin: City of Dublin Vocational Education Committee), 1991.

Street. Soon afterwards, at the request of the Irish Tourist Association, institutional and hotel cookery courses were added, as well as a one-and-a-half year postgraduate course in dietetics. By 1949 the latter course had been transformed into a four-year full-time course, recognised by the British Dietetic Association as fulfilling its academic requirements for membership.

In 1951 the Department of Education and the CDVEC agreed to transfer the domestic science course to St Angela's College, Lough Gill, Co. Sligo and to develop in Cathal Brugha Street college the education and training needed by the embryonic Irish hotel, tourism and catering industry. Within the college, which soon became the College of Catering, the main course areas became dietetics, hotel and catering management, institutional and household management, domestic science, professional cookery and apprentice training for chefs.

From the earliest years, part-time day and evening courses in subjects such as professional cookery, dressmaking, millinery, housecrafts, laundry work and physical culture were an important part of the work of the college.

A two-year hotel and catering course for boys and girls, begun in 1952, became the hotel management course in 1954 and included a six-month placement in the industry immediately after graduation. The apprentice chefs' course had been moved from the Parnell Square school as part of the process of concentrating hotel, tourism and catering education in Cathal Brugha Street college in the early 1950s. It was a course for boys only at the time, but it soon stimulated the development of a parallel course for girls.

Cathal Brugha Street College Principals	
Kathleen O'Sullivan	1941–1950
Winifred Bouchier-Hayes	1951–1969
Gerti Armstrong	1969–1973
Robert J. Lawlor	1973–1993

In 1961 the hotel and catering course in the Cathal Brugha Street college was converted to a three-year full-time diploma course in hotel management and the first graduates emerged in 1965. By 1968 there was a range of other full-time courses in disciplines such as hotel catering, book-keeper/receptionist, hotel cookery, apprentice chefs/cooks and apprentice waiters. At the end of the decade the management of the courses in the hotel and catering discipline was divided into two schools — hotel and catering administration, and hotel and catering operations. In 1973 the household management discipline was constituted into the school of home and social sciences. A school of food technology and environmental health was also established.

A major extension to the college, providing new kitchens and larders, staff and student dining room facilities, a reception area and a students' common room, was completed in January 1966.

Under the partnership agreement with the University of Dublin (see Chapter 4) the Cathal Brugha Street college developed degree courses in hotel and catering management and environmental health after 1976. These and other higher level courses in tourism marketing, early childhood care and education, social studies, hotel management, catering management, hotel reception, travel/tourism, hotel/catering supervision, food technology, food quality assurance and health care technology, are outlined in Chapter 8.

In 1986 a full-time certificate course in culinary arts was developed which focussed on catering for health and by 1999, a primary degree course in this subject was sanctioned by the Department of Education after some controversy. Postgraduate diploma and master's degree courses were developed in the 1990s in hospitality management and rural tourism.

By the 1990s, the Cathal Brugha Street college catered for the following disciplines, most of which have a strong reliance on specialised laboratory, kitchen, restaurant and other facilities: hotel, tourism and catering management, hotel and catering operations, culinary arts, food science and environmental health and home and social sciences. Indeed, during the 1980s the academic structure of the college had been reformed into those four schools.

THE BALLYMUN PROJECT

Higher level education began its major modern expansion in the 1960s. Despite the extension to the Bolton Street college and the acquisition of the Linen Hall premises for a School of Trades in the early 1960s, and the new college in Kevin Street completed in 1967, all the Dublin colleges were greatly restricted in their development by a shortage of accommodation. Their city centre locations offered limited scope for the expansion needed to allow more students and more courses.

In the mid-1960s the CDVEC decided to conduct a detailed study of the long-term needs of the colleges. In October 1964 it appointed an authoritative Planning Subcommittee "to advise it on the needs of the city of Dublin in the field of vocational education and to recommend how these needs should be met. The Subcommittee should have regard also of the national needs in vocational education."

The Planning Subcommittee had the following composition:

Membership of the Planning Subcommittee 1964–1967

Chairman
M. J. Cranley, Director General, Institute for Research and Standards (replaced in 1966 by P. Donegan, Chairman of the CDVEC)

Members
Five members of the CDVEC — J. McCann, J. Barron, Mons. J. O'Regan, S. O'Hanlon and J. A. Kelly
A. Harkin, Chief Engineer, Electricity Supply Board
F. Kennedy, General Secretary, Irish Transport and General Workers' Union
A.K. Mills, Chief Chemist, A. Guinness & Co., Ltd
M. McCourt, Managing Director, General Electric Company (Ireland) Ltd
P. McLoughlin, Mechanical Engineer, Dublin Port and Docks Board
M. M. Gleeson, Chief Executive Officer, CDVEC
H. J. Healy, Principal Officer, CDVEC
D. F. O'Dwyer, Principal, College of Technology, Bolton Street
J. D. Barry, Vice-Principal, College of Technology, Bolton Street
H. de Lacy, Principal, College of Technology, Kevin Street
S. Ó Ceallaigh, Principal, College of Commerce, Rathmines

Advisory and Research Officers
G. Latchford, Vice-Principal, College of Technology, Kevin Street
T. McCarthy, Chief Educational Psychologist, CDVEC

Liaison Officer
T. Ó Grianáin, Senior Inspector, Department of Education

Secretary
J. B. Hickey, Head of School of Trades, Linen Hall

The Planning Subcommittee first reported in 1966 on the second-level sector. Then in an extensive study of the higher education sector, reported on in 1967, it undertook to devise a physical and organisational plan that would allow for growth and technological change in the years ahead. It also placed emphasis on service to the industrial, commercial and other sectors of the community while keeping the best interests of the student as an individual to the forefront. It emphasised education above training in its planning. It also recommended that, in relation to the level of courses to be provided in the colleges, there should, in principle, be no restriction on the level.

In its work the Subcommittee considered the 1967 report of the Commission on Higher Education and the other recent developments in higher education outlined in this and the following chapter.[3] It estimated the needs for different levels of education in the trades, technology, management and commerce and gauged the capacity of the Dublin colleges to provide them. It investigated the availability of suitable sites adjacent to the colleges themselves with a view to providing the required expansion close to the centre of the city. It concluded that the cost of adequate site acquisition adjacent to the colleges would be prohibitive. As a result the Subcommittee recommended that the best long-term solution would be to relocate the higher level programmes in business (from Rathmines) and engineering and construction disciplines (from Bolton Street and Kevin Street) to a new, twenty-four hectare, campus site at Albert College in Ballymun. This site was then being vacated by the Agriculture Faculty of UCD, and was being made available by Dublin Corporation. The college in Kevin Street would be developed for higher level scientific programmes, including paramedical and food science disciplines.

This proposed location was viewed by the Subcommittee, and indeed by the CDVEC, as decidedly less satisfactory than a city centre location. When approved, somewhat reluctantly, by the CDVEC in 1969, these recommendations became known as the Ballymun Project proposals.

Under this proposed plan the new Kevin Street college, together with the Ballymun college — essentially the Dublin New College of the Commission on Higher Education report — would "be integrated to form a single autonomous institution with a single governing board and academic council". The proposal was presented in February 1969 to the Minister for Education, who referred it to the new Higher Education Authority (HEA) for comment and recommendations.

The counterpart of the Ballymun Project proposals was that the Bolton Street college would consolidate apprentice education, drawing in the electrical trade courses from Kevin Street, and providing some craft based technician courses as well. Thus a sharp geographic and administrative

---

3.   Commission on Higher Education 1960–1967, *I. Presentation and Summary of Report* (Baile Átha Cliath: Oifig an tSoláthair), 1967.

divide would be created between the higher level work and the apprentice/craft work. This would be a break with one of the guiding principles of the CDVEC system which sought to offer ladders of opportunity to students more or less under the same roof. It would also greatly reduce what was perceived as a synergism between the programmes of different levels, in which individual staff members worked at the different levels and both staff and students made use of expensive, commonly available facilities. This factor also added to the relative reluctance with which the Subcommittee and the CDVEC accepted the Ballymun Project proposals.

Processing the Ballymun Project proposals

The Ballymun Project proposals represented the CDVEC's effort to provide the physical resources and accommodation for the colleges to develop their higher level work within a unified institution, and to adequately respond to the educational needs then emerging rapidly in Irish society.

The HEA, to which the proposal had been referred by the Minister for Education in 1969, reported back in December 1970 and very positively supported the main thrust of the Ballymun Project proposals with some modifications. However, this report was not published by the HEA until July 1972,[4] and at that time the Minister did not give approval for the project to go ahead. In 1972 also the HEA published a report on university reorganisation.[5] This report gave rise to considerable debate in the universities over the next two years or so, with its proposals for major rationalisation in the two Dublin universities — University College Dublin (UCD) and Trinity College Dublin (TCD) — including the amalgamation of faculties and the transfer of departments and staff between them.

In April 1969, the Dublin City Council together with its subcommittees, including the CDVEC, was dissolved by the Minister for Local Government and, until June 1974, an appointed City Commissioner administered their functions.

After its return to office in June 1974, the CDVEC maintained that the new institution to emerge from the Ballymun Project should be within its remit. The Burke Proposals of 1974, detailed in Chapter 3, did not make direct reference to the Dublin colleges as such or to the Ballymun Project. But the proposal to establish a National Institute of Higher Education (NIHE) in Dublin was generally interpreted as giving approval to the implementation of the CDVEC Ballymun Project proposals that had already

---

4. *Report on the Ballymun Project* (Dublin: Higher Education Authority), 1972.
5. *Report on University Re-Organisation* (Dublin: Higher Education Authority), 1972.

received HEA approval. This was one of the missed opportunities referred to in the introduction. It was due to a misreading of the macro-political agenda by the CDVEC. Some months later, in July 1975, the NIHE Dublin was established on an *ad hoc* basis with its own Governing Body, which had some representation from the CDVEC system, but was independent of it. An NIHE/CDVEC liaison committee was established in mid-1976, with representatives from both the NIHE Governing Body and the CDVEC, to recommend which of the latter's higher level college courses and resources should be transferred to the NIHE.

This consultation revealed a wide range of difficulties associated with the process of dividing the programmes and resources of the colleges. In some colleges there was considerable "vertical" integration in the work of staff members and in the use of expensive equipment and accommodation between the higher level work and the broad apprentice level work. Some amount of subdivision of colleges was envisaged, in a context where the scope for further expansion was limited to begin with. The extent to which this division would damage the long held principle of the colleges of providing vertical ladders of opportunity in educational provision, particularly to the able students, became manifest. The processes of transferring and possibly regrading staff would give rise to tensions in the system. Divisions and misgivings developed among staff, even senior staff and CDVEC members, about the wisdom of proceeding along that road.

By October 1976 no significant progress had been made by the liaison committee and the Minister for Education, Peter Barry TD, established a working party on higher technological education in the Dublin area "to examine and make proposals for the apportionment of levels of academic activity to NIHE Dublin and a new CDVEC institution, in accordance with their respective national and international roles . . . of existing courses in the CDVEC colleges between the two institutions . . . of existing buildings and related physical resources". It was also "to define procedures for the transfer of staff to one or other institution . . . (and) recommend a governing structure for the new CDVEC institution and its relationship to its NIHE counterpart". In general the NIHE would cater for undergraduate and postgraduate courses, diploma courses, some certificate courses relating to the higher level work and adult education. The new CDVEC institution would cater for some diploma courses, as well as certificate courses, craft/apprentice courses and adult education.

The working party reported to the Minister in January 1977 and this report was conveyed to the CDVEC in April of that year.[6] The CDVEC

6. *Report of the Working Party on Higher Technological Education in the Dublin Area to the Minister for Education* (Dublin), 20 December 1976.

conveyed its rejection of the recommendations in this report to the Minister in August 1977. None of the recommendations was ever implemented and no courses or facilities were transferred. The NIHE Dublin was subsequently developed as a greenfield project on the site of the former Albert College in Glasnevin, where the Ballymun Project was to have been located.

INTERNAL REORGANISATION WITHIN THE DUBLIN COLLEGES

While the Ballymun Project proposals were being considered in the Department of Education, related academic and organisational preparations were also being made within the Dublin colleges.

In the earlier years when higher level courses in the colleges were provided to prepare students for the examinations of professional and other external bodies, the responsibility for academic standards and quality assurance was entrusted to the school/department and college conducting the course. Peer review occurred through the mechanism of the external examinations of the professional bodies. Later the colleges broadened the courses to include wider educational objectives and began to set their own examinations and make their own awards. Peer review was now implemented through the moderation of these examinations by external examiners appointed by the colleges. In due course these examinations, and the college awards associated with them, were accepted by professional bodies as meeting their academic requirements for corporate membership. Thus they were accorded the same external recognition as honours degrees from the universities, a very important development.

Since the 1930s the Board of Studies had served as the main means of academic co-ordination between the colleges. With the development of full-time degree level courses, however, and the parallel development of full-time technician courses in the colleges during the 1960s, the CDVEC, in consultation with the management of the colleges, recognised the need for better co-ordination of this activity.

Academic Council

In the late 1960s the Academic Council was established on an *ad hoc* basis by the CDVEC, with a membership expanded beyond that of the Board of Studies to include senior staff members, teaching staff representatives and, much later a co-opted student representative.

By 1970 each of the six colleges was developing along broadly parallel patterns in complementary discipline areas. The Academic Council was formally established by order of the City Commissioner in October 1970 in pursuance of the CDVEC's declared policy, as expressed in the Ballymun Project proposals, of providing a unified third level institution in Dublin.[7] The general function of the Academic Council was to be responsible to the CDVEC, for planning, co-ordinating and developing third level education in the Dublin colleges.

Membership of the Academic Council

The Chief Executive Officer of the CDVEC, together with the principal and assistant principal of each college, were ex-officio members of the Council. Heads of departments whose courses fell largely within the ambit of the Council's general function were also members. On the recommendation of the Council, other members of the academic staffs of the colleges might, from time to time, be appointed to the Council by the CDVEC, to "ensure adequate representation of different areas of academic activity".

The Council was also empowered to invite members of college staffs, students or other persons to attend meetings and to participate in discussions, with the proviso that such persons would not be permitted to vote on any resolution of the Council.

The intention was that when the planned unified third level institution was established, the director would be chairperson of the Academic Council. However, pending that establishment, the chairperson was to be elected by the Academic Council from among its members. This was an effective practice and the election of members from the different colleges to be chairperson at different times helped to develop institutional cohesion.

Terms of reference of the Academic Council

The Academic Council was accountable to the CDVEC under the following terms of reference, for:

• the establishment, maintenance and development of courses, other academic work (including research) and academic standards in the colleges, both individually and on a co-operative basis between colleges

---

7.   *Academic Council* (Dublin: City of Dublin Vocational Education Committee), October 1970.

- academic requirements for the admission of students to and continued participation in such courses
- making awards to persons who had successfully completed courses approved for the purposes of such awards
- the award of scholarships, prizes or other distinctions
- regulation of examinations conducted by the colleges
- appointment of external examiners
- nomination of academic representatives to external bodies
- development and maintenance of liaison with industry, commerce, professional bodies, research organisations and other educational institutions
- the establishment of boards of studies or other committees for academic purposes
- selection of academic staff
- fostering of academic staff development and the establishment of programmes for such development
- other appropriate matters referred to the Council by the CDVEC.

The Academic Council was also empowered to make such reports as it thought fit to the CDVEC on academic or related matters. It also had the authority to delegate particular functions to the academic management of an individual college in matters not affecting the other colleges. Thus the primary objective of the Academic Council was to assist in the maintenance and enhancement of academic standards of the higher level courses and professional diploma courses (by then widely acknowledged as being at honours degree level), and also the two-year and three-year full-time technician courses that had recently been developed in a range of discipline areas. The Academic Council was also entrusted with the promotion of research and development work and staff development in the different colleges through co-operation and sharing of expertise and resources.

In today's terminology the Academic Council was established with a remit that specifically included academic quality assurance and quality enhancement. Its work became widely accepted and respected by the academic communities in the different colleges. The establishment of the office of Academic Registrar, the function of which was to support the work of the Council and provide a co-ordinating service to the colleges and their departments, assisted the work of the Academic Council.

Balance sheet of the work of the Academic Council

The Academic Council failed over the years to achieve a "fully integrated third-level Institute" or a "fully integrated apprentice Institute". In each case it could be argued that the authority of the college principals in their position as the legal officer was a major impediment to that integration. Neither was the large and fairly unwieldy Academic Council an effective instrument for such organisational integration. It was not an executive body. Nevertheless, in the area of broad academic quality assurance, it achieved considerable advances and unity of approach across the colleges.

ESTABLISHMENT OF THE DUBLIN INSTITUTE OF TECHNOLOGY

The response of the CDVEC to the outcome of the Ballymun Project proposals was to establish the Dublin Institute of Technology (DIT) on an *ad hoc* basis in 1978. The function of the DIT was to further co-ordinate the work of the six colleges and their College Councils, and indeed to help manage the partnership agreement with the University of Dublin that had been signed in 1976 (see Chapter 4). At the time the CDVEC viewed the DIT as the next organic phase in the progress of the Dublin colleges.[8] A Governing Body was formed with a more broadly based membership than the CDVEC itself. It included representation from staff and other interests. The individual College Councils, the Academic Council and the Apprentice Education Board all reported to it rather than to the parent CDVEC. It was given the dual remit of co-ordinating the work of the colleges as well as focussing on more general policy issues affecting the development of the Institute. Mr Hugh de Lacy, then principal of the Kevin Street college, was appointed as chairperson of the newly formed Executive Council (the principals of the six colleges) and director of the DIT in an *ad hoc* capacity. He served until his retirement in 1981. In 1982 he was replaced by Mr Michael O'Donnell, then principal of the Bolton Street college, who served on a similar basis until 1993.

CDVEC policy document on the unification of the colleges

The following memorandum of 1978 set out the role and functions given to the DIT Governing Body by CDVEC.[9]

---

8.   Donegan, P, *Opening of Academic Year 1978/1979 Address by Chairman CDVEC* (Dublin: City of Dublin Vocational Education Committee), September 1978.
9.   *For Information of the Staffs of the Colleges: Unification of the Third-Level Colleges* (Dublin: City of Dublin Vocational Education Committee), 25 May 1978.

The Committee at its meeting, 25 May 1978, made the following order in relation to its third level colleges. This order, which will have effect from 1 September 1978, is intended to commence the process of unification of the CDVEC colleges.

The new Institute would be called "The Dublin Institute of Technology".

The Institute would be set up under section 21 of the Vocational Education Act 1930.

In accordance with Section 21 of the Act the Governing Body of the Institute will consist of 12 people:
• six Committee members
• two members from industry and commerce
• one representative of the Dublin Council of Trade Unions
• one student
• one chairman of the executive council
• one staff representative.

The number of people who would normally attend the Governing Body meeting would not exceed twenty-five. There would be twelve voting members and thirteen (other) members in attendance. The members in attendance would include the CEO, the remaining college principals, the Academic Registrar, chairmen of various sub-committees, such as Academic Council, etc.

The Governing Body shall have responsibility for:
(a) the running of the Institute
(b) the development of a fully integrated third level Institute
(c) the development of a fully integrated apprentice Institute.

The Institute's Executive Council shall consist of the college principals one of whom will be elected chairman of the Executive Council and director of the Institute. The term of the director of the Institute shall not exceed three years at any one time, and may be renewable for another one year. Thereinafter that member of the Executive Council must stand down for at least one further term (i.e. three years). As the name implies the Institute's Executive would have executive powers and the director of the Institute and chairman of the Executive Council would in fact, be the director of the Institute.

The Institute's Governing Body would in the normal course of events appoint a number of subcommittees that would report through the Executive Council to the Governing Body.

The existing College Councils would act as Advisory Councils to the various subgroupings within the Institute and the minutes of the College Council would be passed in the normal way through the Executive Council to the Governing Body.

INITIAL DEVELOPMENT OF THE DUBLIN INSTITUTE OF TECHNOLOGY

The Irish higher education system continued to grow in the 1980s and the statutory framework for the system was also developed to accommodate it. The DIT made a major contribution to that growth. It continued to develop and integrate, particularly in its internal academic and management structures. Despite continuing constraints and limitations of accommodation and other resources, the DIT responded to the large and relatively unsatisfied demand from school leavers seeking full-time courses and from apprentices already in employment wishing to enrol on part-time courses. A number of options were explored including leasing office accommodation and industrial factory buildings adjacent to the colleges. Some such measures were taken to provide short-term solutions. As is apparent from Tables 8.1 to 8.5, several new programmes were established in response to student demand and the numbers of staff and full-time students (Table 8.6) in the colleges increased significantly. Management structures were reformed and the levels of the college facilities and equipment were enhanced during this period.

Governing Body review of the DIT in 1983

In February 1983, the Governing Body carried out a general review of the operation of the Institute, including identifying a number of weaknesses and projecting its future development.[10] It reiterated the overall objective of a single unified institution with greater sharing of resources and interaction between different sections. It saw as necessary the diminution of the autonomy of the individual colleges and the need for principals and heads of school to identify with the DIT rather than with their individual colleges. It considered very desirable the sharing of courses and of staff and resources, and also the elimination of unjustified duplication and non-

---

10. *Report on Governing Body Seminar* (Dublin: City of Dublin Vocational Education Committee), February, 1983.

viable courses. It suggested that the Institute's image should be promoted through unified DIT prospectuses, graduation ceremonies and publicity material. In particular it strongly supported the establishment of a faculty structure to co-ordinate related disciplines across the Institute. It agreed to work towards harmonising student admissions, student records, examination procedures and regulations. It also agreed to give attention to:

- greater provision of part-time courses, including part-time versions of full-time courses
- development of the transfer ladders to allow students to progress to higher levels
- facilitating entry to students from CDVEC second level schools through transition courses
- greater provision of continuing education, short course and adult education courses.

It saw the need for improved staff and student accommodation throughout the colleges and better sports and recreational facilities as well.

Some of these desirable improvements and reforms were indeed implemented as resources became available, but many were not. In particular the unification and integration of the colleges into a unitary DIT was not fully successful. Nevertheless, the Governing Body showed itself to be critically aware of the key issues in the Institute and capable of pointing to reasonable solutions. However, it might be argued that the CDVEC did not pursue these solutions with sufficient persistence and vigour during the latter part of the 1980s. This may have been for reasons associated with the new legislation for the DIT intimated in the Green Paper on education in 1985 (see Chapter 3).[11]

College-based organisational structure

The individual colleges evolved organically over many years under the aegis of the CDVEC. Since the early 1960s each college had its own College Council reporting to the CDVEC and, in more recent times, to the DIT Governing Body. Each college developed its own range of courses, relating to its existing disciplines, and each had its own principal and administrative/academic structure. It generated its own ethos, individuality and character.

---

11. *Partners in Education: Serving Community Needs* (Baile Átha Cliath: Oifig an tSoláthair), 1985.

While it was evident that there was some overlap between disciplines operating in different colleges, these were tolerated. Although the Academic Council, established formally in 1970, carried out an important academic co-ordinating function in relation to course validation and standards, there was little co-operation between the colleges involving sharing of resources or joint course development. This might be considered another missed opportunity, the effects of which are continuing to the present.

Schools and departments in the colleges

Within each college there were a number of mainly discipline-based schools or departments. The use of the terms "school" and "department" was not uniform throughout the Institute. Until the 1990s, in the Kevin Street and Bolton Street colleges, the main constituent parts were "departments", generally headed by a person at Senior Lecturer II (SL II) grade, although some of the smaller "departments" were headed by persons at Senior Lecturer I (SL I) grade. Many of the "departments" in these two colleges were large units, responsible for a number of courses and several hundred students, with an academic management substructure comprising one or more assistant heads at SL I grade. In the other colleges the main units were described as "schools", also generally headed by persons at SL II grade, but often with subunits described as "departments" headed by persons at SL I grade. These anomalies of nomenclature have been addressed in recent years and, in the new system being developed, the basic unit will be called the "school", headed by a person at SL III grade (a restructuring from SL II agreed in 1999). A school may have subdivision(s) called departments, headed by persons at SL II grade (also restructured from SL I in 1999).

Academic management of each college

Each college functioned as an academic unit under the management of the principal. Individual colleges had developed different internal committee structures to suit their requirements. Each college also had a college Management or Executive Board consisting of the principal and the senior staff (mostly SL II) to advise the principal and assist in the general management of the college.

In relation to many programmes of study there was considerable collaboration between schools and departments in the design and delivery of courses, but mainly within colleges. This collaboration involved a shared management of a course assisted by a Course Committee, or the provision of service teaching by one school/department to a course for which another school/department was primarily responsible.

General staffing of each college

The recruitment of academic staff was initiated and processed by the individual colleges through the personnel section of the CDVEC, which organised advertisements and interviews. The staff members, when appointed, were attached to particular schools or departments, which were then responsible for their initiation and deployment. The CDVEC personnel section was then primarily concerned with staff salaries, incremental credit, pension arrangements, monitoring sick leave and interacting with trade unions.

Each college had a core administrative staff to provide local services in relation to finance and accounts, student registration, student records, examination administration and other administrative matters relating to equipment and materials acquisition and provision of services. There was, however, considerable transfer of administrative staff between colleges, which also had a general support staff including technicians, laboratory aides, porters and other security staff. In most cases, maintenance, cleaning and restaurant services were provided through a contract arrangement.

Each college also had its own library under the management of a qualified librarian, who reported to the local principal and was assisted by a number of other staff. The Public Library Service of Dublin Corporation employed the librarians and this body also provided certain support services in relation to book acquisition and cataloguing. There was a central DIT Library Committee, which in recent years has been made a subcommittee of the Academic Council, with representation from each college and this helped in co-ordinating the overall service.

Summary

In the newly independent Saorstát Éireann, the Dublin colleges helped to shape the Vocational Education Act 1930 and then proceeded to steadily plan and develop their services within the CDVEC, under the aegis of that legislation. Under the Apprenticeship Act 1931 the colleges pioneered the provision of the educational elements of apprenticeship training in a wide range of disciplines, including non-designated trades.

From the 1930s the CDVEC also developed plans for the delivery of co-ondinated higher education programmes in the colleges. Therefore, as

long ago as the 1930s the earliest plans for a higher technological education Institute in the centre of Dublin were formed. The strategic vision
guiding the plans of the time laid the foundations and defined the characteristics and policies of the Institute in the years that followed. This vision
included:

- autonomy and the power to grant diploma awards
- clear differentiation between higher level and lower (second) level work
- city centre locations
- a vocational and applied orientation
- comprehensive coverage of technical and business disciplines
- links with the professional bodies
- co-operation with industry/commerce
- specially trained teachers
- research for industry
- responsiveness to the needs of industry.

Although these strategies were not fully implemented at the time, the Dublin
colleges pioneered the involvement of educational institutions in apprentice training. As a result they helped to elevate the quality of apprentice-
ships in Ireland. Through interaction, collaboration and consultation with
industry and the professions, they managed to develop a multi-level range
of courses, by reorienting flexibly to the changing needs in society, and
generally by being guided by the educational and training needs of society.

The early 1960s heralded the beginnings of the modern expansion in
higher education in Ireland, strongly supported by government policies
and funding. Each of the Dublin colleges, under the aegis of the CDVEC,
contributed to providing courses to meet the demand from increasing numbers of students. The Ballymun Project proposals, with roots in the CDVEC
thinking of the 1930s, formed the most extensive and ambitious planning
process ever undertaken by the Dublin colleges. The proposals steered
them towards developing a unitary multi-level higher education institution and, more clearly than ever before, to solving their accommodation
needs definitively as the optimum response to the needs of the renascent
Dublin and Irish economy.

The development and growth of higher education in Ireland in the 1970s
led to increased government involvement, as well as to increased uncertainty and disquiet within the higher education institutions. In the Dublin
colleges, the Academic Council, which had been set up in the late 1960s

on an *ad hoc* basis, was formally established in 1970 to oversee its higher education programmes. It served to improve the integration of the colleges, raise the level of the academic activities and introduce quality assurance procedures.

The Ballymun Project proposals were a bold initiative designed to help solve the perennial problem in the colleges of inadequate accommodation for the numbers of students seeking to avail of their programmes. In some respects the proposals contained the seeds of their own destruction. Certainly, if the Dublin colleges had been more positively involved in the National Council for Educational Awards (NCEA) system by that stage, they might have been in a better position politically to gain the Albert College site for the Ballymun Project. As it was, the government decided to develop a greenfield NIHE on the site, independent of the CDVEC. In this defeat, however, the CDVEC formed the DIT on an *ad hoc* basis in 1978. The DIT's mission was to unify the Dublin colleges under the aegis of the CDVEC. The Institute was given a Governing Body responsible to the CDVEC and an Academic Council responsible to this Governing Body. This DIT was envisaged as a multi-level, fully integrated, third level institution, incorporating higher level and apprentice education. In many ways this was an inspirational way to finish a turbulent, roller-coaster decade of development for the Dublin colleges.

The 1980s saw some enhancement of the facilities and accommodation in the DIT colleges — unfortunately always too little and too late to match the demand. The integration and consolidation of the Institute continued. But the strong identity of the individual colleges and their reputation in their specialist areas continued to influence the externally perceived image of the DIT. Full-time student numbers grew particularly in this decade. The positive effect of the partnership agreement with the University of Dublin contributed to increased numbers on primary degree courses. There was also strong enrolment in courses leading to DIT's own diploma and certificate awards. Increasing numbers of DIT students were pursuing postgraduate research, although registering and graduating in universities in Ireland and abroad.

Chapter 3

Government Policy and Legislative Backdrop to the Emergence of the DIT

At the time of independence in 1922, the administration of technical/vocational education in Ireland fell within the remit of the Department of Agriculture and Technical Instruction. In 1924, however, after the establishment of Saorstát Éireann (Irish Free State), technical education was assigned to the newly established Department of Education. Since then the government has developed its involvement in higher education through official commissions of inquiry and other published studies, green (discussion) papers and white (policy) papers leading to appropriate legislation. This chapter presents a digest of this development from a DIT perspective.

COMMISSION OF INQUIRY (TECHNICAL EDUCATION) 1926

The Minister for Education set up an advisory commission in 1926 to enquire into the technical education system, particularly in relation to the needs of trade and industry. The international membership of this commission of inquiry is given below:

Members of the Commission of Inquiry 1926

Chairman:
J. Ingram, Senior Inspector of Technical Education

Members:
A. Rohn, President, Federal Polytechnicum, Zürich
N. Fredricksson, Board of Education, Sweden
J. Good, TD
H. Colohan, TD
J. J. O'Connor, Headmaster, Technical School, Mallow
B. Stafford, Department of Industry and Commerce
W. Doolin, Principal Officer, Department of Finance
T. O'Connell, Senior Agricultural Inspector, Department of Lands and Agriculture

---

The City of Dublin Technical Education Committee (TEC) and the Rathmines Technical Instruction Committee (TIC) each made detailed submissions to the commission.[1] They formulated strong arguments in relation to the value of technical education to the new state, gave a description of the courses and activities of the schools and institutes under their aegis and, in particular, made suggestions as to how to remove obstacles to progress. Thus, for instance, the City of Dublin TEC listed the chief problems facing it as the deficiencies in primary education, the scarcity of employment for students and graduates, the limited number of industries and the limitations (of amount and location) of its accommodation to satisfy the demand.

The Commission's recommendations were largely incorporated into the Vocational Education Act 1930 and the Apprenticeship Act 1931.[2] Both of these pieces of legislation were to prove enlightened and far-reaching, allowing and generally facilitating the developments in technical education which took place in the Irish vocational education system.

VOCATIONAL EDUCATION ACT 1930

The Vocational Education Act 1930 defined the scope of technical education to include "education pertaining to trades, manufactures, agriculture, commerce and other industrial pursuits" and science, art, music and physical training. It also covered the area of continuation education — "general and practical training in preparation for employment ... and also general and practical training for improvement of young people in the early stages of employment". These stipulations were of much broader scope than had previously been the case.

In order to implement the legislation throughout the country, thirty-eight Vocational Education Committees (VECs) were established by the County Councils and certain designated urban district authorities. These VECs were therefore subcommittees of the local rating (taxing) authority and were funded by a combination of central government and local rates contributions.

---

1. Hernon, PJ, *Statement of Evidence* (Dublin: City of Dublin Technical Education Committee), 1926; Clampett, G J T, *Summary of Evidence submitted to the Commission of Enquiry into Technical Education* (Dublin: Rathmines Technical Instruction Committee), 1926.
2. *Report of the Commission of Inquiry (Technical Education)* (Baile Átha Cliath: Oifig an tSoláthair), 1927.

The Act gave wide powers to VECs to organise courses at different levels in response to local demands. The Act also encouraged co-operation between the local VEC and employers' bodies to establish educational and training programmes necessary to equip young people for the developing needs of the Irish economy.

As mentioned in the previous chapter, the City of Dublin Vocational Education Committee (CDVEC) became responsible after 1930 for the existing Technical Institutes in Dublin located at Kevin Street, Chatham Row and Bolton Street, and other technical schools including that at Rutland/Parnell Square. The Greater Dublin Act 1930 brought the urban districts of Rathmines and Pembroke into the city, and this brought the Rathmines Technical Institute and the Pembroke Technical and Fishery School at Ringsend into the CDVEC in 1932.

COMMISSION ON HIGHER EDUCATION 1960–1967

The relaxation of trade protectionism, and the opening-up of the economy in the early 1960s and its subsequent growth, were to have profound implications for the higher education system in the Republic of Ireland. One of the first indications of the expansion and of the increasing government involvement to come, happened in the National University of Ireland (NUI). A commission to advise on the accommodation needs of the colleges of the NUI was appointed by the Minister for Education in 1957. In 1959, the commission recommended a major government investment programme — a new £8 million building programme for University College Dublin (UCD) which led to the development of its campus at Belfield, and a £600,000 building programme for each of University College Cork (UCC) and University College Galway (UCG).[3]

In 1960, the government established a Commission on Higher Education, whose membership is given below, "to inquire into and make recommendations in relation to university, professional, technological and higher education generally".[4] The Commission was also directed to give attention to "the general organisation and administration of education at those levels and the nature and extent of the provision to be made for such education".

3.　Commission on University Accommodation 1957–1959, *Report* (Baile Átha Cliath: Oifig an tSoláthair), 1959.
4.　Commission on Higher Education 1960–1967, *I. Presentation and Summary of Report, op. cit.*

Members of the Commission on Higher Education 1960–1967

Chairman:
Cearbhall Ó Dálaigh

Members:
C. S. Andrews, Managing Director, Córas Iompair Éireann; D. Buckley;
H. Butterfield; S. Ó Cadhla; C. F. Carter; Phillis Bean Uí Cheallaigh;
Máirín Bean Uí Chinnéide, scríbhneoir agus léirmheastóir; M. J.
Costello, Managing Director, Comhlacht Siúicre Éireann; M. J. Cranley,
Principal, College of Technology, Kevin Street; J. Dempsey; S. S. de
Faoite; L. Ó Gotharaigh; J. N. Greene; Mr Griffin; S. Ó Lideadha; L. Ó
Luanaigh; E. O'Malley; J. J. McElligott; J. J. McHenry; P. S. Mac
Lochlainn; J. Mitchell; T. W. Moody; P. G. Murphy; R. Gordon Perdue;
W. J. Philbin, Bishop of Down and Connor; T. Walsh

Secretary:
S. Ó Cathail, Department of Education

Assistant Secretary:
L. Ó Fearghail, Department of Education

After extensive inquiries in Ireland and abroad, the Commission reported
in 1967. In its report, the Commission drew attention to the role of the
government as the principal provider of finance to the higher education
institutions. It highlighted the lack of an overall planning authority for
higher education and concluded that essentially no coherent planning was
carried out within the sector. It noted that higher education outside the
universities had "remained comparatively under-developed". It drew attention to academic weaknesses in the universities at undergraduate level
due to "increasing numbers of students, low entry standards and inadequate staffing and accommodation", and at postgraduate research level.
The Commission also called for improvements in university governance
and academic appointment procedures.

Although the Commission emphasised the government's support for
the autonomy of the universities, the government exerted considerable
control over the higher education institutions outside the university sector. Also it saw it as necessary to impose certain limitations to the autonomy of the universities, particularly where the institutions received
large subventions of public funds. The report clearly expressed a dilemma
for the government — it was the authority for deciding on the amounts of
public funds to be devoted to higher education, and yet, in a situation of
institutional autonomy, it had only limited control over how such funds

were utilised. The Commission proposed that a planning and regulating agency be established to provide a buffer between the institutions and the government, similar to the University Grants Commission (UGC) in Britain. This agency would not only plan and administer the state grants to the institutions, but would also be a comprehensive planning authority to preside over the planning and expansion of higher education, then already underway, in order to adequately serve the needs of the country.

The report of the Commission on Higher Education also made important recommendations concerning the activities of the Dublin colleges and their future development. In relation to higher technological education, the Commission recommended the establishment of a technological authority to encompass the work of the Institute for Industrial Research and Standards (the national industrial standards authority) and be responsible for technological education and training. It would also provide technological innovation and foresight information and guidance for industry. It would organise and co-ordinate technological research as well. This technological authority's educational functions would be at the organisational rather than the teaching level, but it would provide scholarships, arrange for academic, training and research programmes and have the power to make academic awards.

In its report the Commission recognised the role of the Dublin colleges in relation to higher technician training and the provision of professional courses. It recommended that the system should continue to "devise courses to meet the specific needs of the country". In particular it recommended that the general and academic management of the higher level work in the colleges should be "established on a quasi-independent basis" and that the Colleges of Technology and the College of Commerce, either collectively or individually, should be given a governing body and an academic type of administration. The colleges and their staff would be engaged in schemes of industrial and technological training and research. Their work would, in general, be complementary to that of the universities.

This was the first recommendation for the development of a binary approach to higher education in Ireland — a university system and on the other side of a 'binary divide', a complementary 'technological' system. Such a system had been developed in Britain in the mid-1960s, for the quite different economic, social, political and educational conditions there. It would appear that the concept was imported with a minimum of modification or matching to conditions in Ireland. In subsequent years it blossomed into the policy of the Department of Education.

In relation to music, the Commission recommended that the Dublin

Municipal School of Music should combine its higher level work with that of the Royal Irish Academy of Music to form the music department of a proposed New College in Dublin.

Indeed a number of New Colleges, distributed among the regions of the country, were recommended, within a clear binary concept of higher education. The New Colleges would function in the humanistic, commercial and scientific fields. They would offer three-year full-time courses or equivalent part-time courses with a strong vocational bias and leading to awards of pass or general degree standard.

The Commission's report strongly recommended that the various institutions of higher education should develop formal relationships with each other, particularly in areas of mutual interest and common activity.

THE O'MALLEY PROPOSALS FOR UNIVERSITY REFORM

Soon after the publication of the report of the Commission, the Minister for Education, Donogh O'Malley TD, made a controversial speech in December 1967, in which he declared the policy of the government to reorganise University College Dublin (UCD) and Trinity College Dublin (TCD) into a single university.[5] This merger proposal generated high emotion in both universities.

A government policy statement was issued in July 1968, which proposed the dissolution of the NUI and the establishment of UCC and UCG as independent universities. It proposed that in the merged Dublin university with one governing body, UCD and TCD would retain their identities with their own councils and would each have an allocation of faculties and schools to improve efficiency. The statement also announced the government's decision to establish the Higher Education Authority (HEA) to deal with planning and financing in higher education as recommended by the Commission on Higher Education.

STEERING COMMITTEE ON TECHNICAL EDUCATION 1966–1969

As the Irish economy developed in the 1960s, it became clear to the government that it needed to provide higher education to cater for the manpower requirements of industrial development. While Dublin, Cork, Limerick and possibly Galway were catered for to some extent by the univer-

---

5. Coolahan, J, *Irish Education: History and Structure, op. cit.*

sities and local colleges, there was a general shortage of appropriately skilled and qualified personnel throughout the regions of the country. As evidenced by the OECD studies in the 1960s, there was also need to provide apprentice and technician training in the regions outside the cities not serviced by higher education.[6]

In 1964 the Minister for Education, Patrick Hillery TD, announced the government's proposal to locate "ten regional technical colleges (RTCs) ... [in] Dublin with two centres, Cork and Limerick ... [and] Waterford, Galway, Dundalk, Sligo, Athlone, Carlow".[7] In 1966 the government appointed a Steering Committee on Technical Education. This committee made two reports, one in 1967 and the second in 1969. In close parallel with developments in the binary system in Britain at the time, it recommended that a national body be established to co-ordinate developments within the RTCs and that each college should be controlled regionally.[8] Each RTC was established under the relevant vocational education committee. The National Council for Educational Awards (NCEA), established in 1972 as a validation and awards body, provided overall academic guidance and co-ordination. The Steering Committee envisaged that the RTCs would provide courses aimed at filling deficiencies in industrial manpower requirements, especially at technician level, and it suggested also that they should be flexible to respond to social, economic and technological needs in their regions.

The plans for the Dublin RTCs were not implemented. Lobbying in Limerick resulted in the establishment there, in 1969, of the first National Institute for Higher Education (NIHE) which became the University of Limerick (UL) in 1989. The NIHE Dublin was established on an *ad hoc* basis in 1974 and became Dublin City University (DCU) in 1989. The RTCs were established as follows: Athlone, Carlow, Dundalk, Sligo and Waterford in 1970, Letterkenny in 1971, Galway in 1972, Cork in 1974 and Tralee in 1977. Following the RTC Act 1992, the Limerick College of Art, Commerce and Technology was designated an RTC. The Tallaght RTC opened in 1992, the Dún Laoghaire RTC was constituted in 1998 and the Blanchardstown Institute of Technology began in 1999. All the RTCs were designated Institutes of Technology in 1998.

---

6. *Investment in Education* (Paris: OECD), 1962; *Training of Technicians in Ireland* (Paris: OECD), 1964.
7. MacKeogh, K, 'The Regional Technical Colleges and the Changing Geography of Higher Education in the Republic of Ireland', *Irish Geography*, XVI, 121, 1983.
8. Godwin, CD, 'The Origin of the Binary System', *History of Education*, 27/2, 171–91, 1998.

HIGHER EDUCATION AUTHORITY ACT 1971

In response to the 1967 report of the Commission on Higher Education, the government set up the HEA on an *ad hoc* basis in 1968. It was formally established under the provisions of the Higher Education Authority Act 1971, which set out its functions. Among these functions were "the development of higher education" and "the promotion of the attainment of equality of opportunity in higher education and the democratisation of its structures". The direct remit and funding role of the HEA included assigning its block grants to the universities and other designated institutions. It was also given advisory powers in relation to the full range of higher level education provision.

The universities themselves were given almost complete autonomy over internal distribution of resources allocated to them from the government through the HEA. Since its inception, the HEA has continued to facilitate the general autonomy and academic freedom of the institutions under its aegis. Nevertheless, in the context of its advisory powers, the HEA, as it was established, failed to address a number of the concerns of the Commission on Higher Education in relation to standards and quality of programmes within the institutions. Indeed, not until the discussions leading to the Universities Act 1997 were quality assurance issues, as cited in the report of the Commission, addressed at the legislative level. Neither has the HEA meaningfully addressed the "full range of higher education", being almost solely concerned with the universities and designated institutions over the years. For instance, it has not considered issues such as the utility and suitability of the binary system in higher education in Ireland, particularly in the context of the democratisation of structures in society.

CENTRAL APPLICATIONS OFFICE 1977

A points system was first introduced in the National University of Ireland in 1970 in the situation of more applicants for courses than the numbers of places available.[9] The idea was to systematically select a quota of students from the eligible applicants, normally with Leaving Certificate qualifications.

In 1977 a number of the universities set up a central points system

---

9.   Commission on the Points System, *Consultative Process – Background Document* (Baile Átha Cliath: Oifig na tSoláthair), 1998.

which was administered on their behalf by a Central Applications Office (CAO). Until 1991, the CAO system catered for degree courses in the universities and other institutions, including the DIT. In parallel, the DIT and the RTCs individually operated similar but separate systems for allocating places on diploma and certificate courses. In 1991 a common application and allocation system for such courses in these institutions — the Central Application System (CAS) — was introduced and administered in parallel with the original CAO degree course system by the CAO.

Between 1991 and 1996 the parallel CAS and CAO application and allocation systems were operated. In 1997 the CAS designation was removed and now the two parallel systems are operated under the single CAO designation.

The basic points allocation system related to performance in the Leaving Certificate examination, and as it stood in 1997 is shown in Table 4.1.

Table 4.1: The Points Allocation System in 1997		
Leaving Certificate Grade	Higher Paper	Ordinary Paper
A1	100	60
A2	90	50
B1	85	45
B2	80	40
B3	75	35
C1	70	30
C2	65	25
C3	60	20
D1	55	15
D2	50	10
D3	45	5

NATIONAL COUNCIL FOR EDUCATIONAL AWARDS ACT 1979

The Commission on Higher Education in 1967 recommended the establishment of what it termed "New Colleges" in Limerick and Dublin. About the time of the inception of the HEA in 1968, the Minister for Education referred to it the "question of establishing a body which would award national qualifications at technician and technologist levels". The following year, in a report entitled *A National Council for Awards and a College of Higher Education at Limerick*, the HEA recommended the establishment of a National Council for Educational Awards (NCEA). This Council would have the power "to grant certificates, diplomas and degrees to persons who have successfully pursued courses of study at third-level educational institutions other than universities". In response the Government established the NCEA on an *ad hoc* basis in 1972.

At that stage, the NCEA became involved in validating some of the Dublin colleges' technician certificate and diploma courses. In fact, about half of the awards made by the NCEA in 1972 were in respect of these courses. Further applications were made in 1973 and 1974 in respect of a number of other courses in the Dublin colleges, including some at professional level for which NCEA degree awards were sought. However, not all the Dublin colleges participated in the NCEA project and the new Academic Council failed to achieve a united view on the matter. Some colleges, particularly the Kevin Street college, objected to such participation, claiming that since the college already had well established and recognised certificate and diploma awards, the value of those awards might be diminished by being accredited by a new, untested and recently established agency.

Initially the NCEA concentrated on processing and approving the large number of technician courses that were coming forward, particularly from the new RTCs, and slow progress was made in validating courses leading to degree awards.

Seven years later, the National Council for Educational Awards Act 1979 was enacted and the NCEA was given statutory powers to provide for national educational awards — degrees, diplomas and certificates — in a range of designated non-university institutions in Ireland. At that point these institutions included the National College of Art and Design in Dublin, the NIHEs in Limerick and Dublin, the Dublin colleges of the CDVEC, Thomond College of Education in Limerick and all the RTCs.

Significantly, the NCEA was given a range of quality assurance functions, although not explicitly identified as such, in respect of its designated institutions. According to the Act, the NCEA could recognise a degree, diploma, certificate or other educational award granted to persons who successfully completed specific approved courses, as well as grant degrees, diplomas, certificates and other educational awards to persons who successfully completed courses approved by the Council. It could approve of such courses of study or instruction. It could also assess the standard maintained by any designated institution. Thus, the NCEA was empowered to:

• accredit institutions

• validate and review programmes of study

• ensure that approved courses had equivalent standards to similar courses in the universities

• confer awards.

From its inception the NCEA developed quality assurance procedures based on the accreditation of institutions, the initial validation, the periodic review of courses and the appointment of external examiners in respect of those examinations moderated by the NCEA for its awards.[10] As these procedures evolved, they included procedures for the appointment of external examiners, the functions and responsibilities of these external examiners *vis-à-vis* internal examiners and examination boards, and the role of the NCEA itself.

It could be argued that the ambivalent attitude of the Dublin colleges to the NCEA was a missed opportunity by these colleges to engage fully with the NCEA project thus lessening its impact at national level. It might also have restricted the potential development of the DIT as well by a failure to develop stronger national links. Certainly, had the Dublin colleges brought their considerable background and experience at every academic level (from apprenticeship training to diploma and degree courses) into the NCEA in a constructive fashion, they could have facilitated the academic and organisational development of the nascent RTC system, and underpinned and confirmed the academic standing of the national awards given by the NCEA. In defence of the leadership of the Dublin colleges in the early 1970s, however, it should be pointed out that they were at that same time engaged in pursuing the Ballymun Project proposals which certainly mapped out a clear alternative path of development. In this context they probably missed the broad, national opportunity for a more narrow and local perspective.

However if the DIT had fully participated in the NCEA project, it might not have achieved the partnership with the University of Dublin (see Chapter 4), or separate legislation from the RTCs (see Chapter 5). Also it might not have been granted the power to award degrees which the RTCs have not yet attained (see Chapter 11). The removal of degree awarding power from the NCEA by the government in 1974 did not enhance the attractiveness of the NCEA to the DIT colleges. This was also a factor in the development of the partnership agreement with the University of Dublin.

---

10. *Examinations Marks and Standards 1998* (Dublin: National Council for Educational Awards), 1998.

NATIONAL INSTITUTE OF HIGHER EDUCATION, LIMERICK 1969

The National Institute of Higher Education (NIHE), Limerick, was established in 1969, as the second part of the response to the HEA report *A National Council for Educational Awards and a College of Higher Education at Limerick*. The plan was for its graduates to receive NCEA awards. This happened until 1974, when the government temporarily withdrew degree awarding power from the NCEA. In that year, the NIHE was accredited for degree awards by the NUI. In 1976 the NIHE Limerick was made a recognised college of the NUI.

BURKE PROPOSALS ON UNIVERSITY REFORM

In December 1974, the Minister for Education, Richard Burke TD, announced his government's decisions and plans in relation to a range of aspects of Irish higher education that had been highlighted in the HEA's *Report on University Reorganisation* in 1972. These proposals contained strong echoes of the O'Malley proposals of seven years before. They constituted a comprehensive set of radical changes and reforms to the higher education system, but were probably less radical than those in the HEA report. These plans are worth outlining here. They became known as the Burke proposals[11] and were as follows:

- there were to be three universities in the state, namely, a university to be constituted from UCD, the University of Dublin (TCD), and the NUI, comprising University College Cork (UCC) and University College Galway (UCG)
- St Patrick's College, Maynooth, was to be given the option of becoming a constituent college of any one of the three universities
- the NIHE Limerick was to be a recognised college of the NUI with the capacity to evolve into a constituent college of the NUI, or become an autonomous institution
- the NIHE Dublin (still to be established) would be a recognised college of either of the Dublin universities with the capacity to evolve into a constituent college of one or another of the Dublin universities, or become an autonomous degree awarding institution
- the majority of the members of the Governing Bodies of the NIHEs in

---

11. Burke, R, TD, Minister for Education, *Proposals of the Government in Relation to Higher Education* (Dublin), December 1974.

Limerick and Dublin were to be nominated by the government, on the recommendation of the Minister for Education, and would include representatives from the trade unions, agriculture, business, industry and educational interests

- a Council for Technological Education was to be established to plan and co-ordinate courses and validate and award non-degree third-level qualifications in the NIHEs in Dublin and Limerick and in the RTCs. This Council was to consist of a Chairman and thirty members. One-third of its membership was to be constituted from and by the Governing Body of the NIHE Limerick, one-third from and by the Governing Body of the NIHE Dublin, and the remaining one-third nominated by the Government on the recommendation of the Minister for Education

- the RTCs would be funded by the Department of Education, in consultation with the Council for Technological Education and through the relevant Vocational Education Committees (VECs)

- a Conjoint Board would be established to co-ordinate the two Dublin universities, with a view to ensuring rational use of resources and mobility of staff and students between them

- the Royal College of Surgeons in Ireland was to remain autonomous but would be brought into the ambit of the Conjoint Board

- a Conference of Irish Universities was to be established

- the following additional bodies were to be designated institutions for the purpose of the Higher Education Authority Act, namely: Conjoint Board of the Dublin universities; Council for Technological Education; NIHEs Dublin and Limerick; Dublin Institute for Advanced Studies; St Patrick's College of Education, Drumcondra; Our Lady of Mercy College of Education, Carysfort Park, Blackrock, Dublin; Church of Ireland College of Education, Rathmines; National College of Art and Design, Dublin; College of Education for Teachers of Specialist Subjects, Limerick; National College of Physical Education, Limerick; Mary Immaculate College of Education, Limerick

- there would be two dental schools in the state, one in Dublin and one in Cork

- the distribution of university faculties in Dublin would be as follows: each university was to have separate faculties of arts, law and pre-clinical medicine; the two universities would share a joint science faculty; there would also be a joint clinical medicine school, operating in three hospital centres and under the direction of the Conjoint Board referred to above; UCD would have faculties of engineering and architecture and TCD a faculty of engineering science but without capital invest-ment; the faculties of business studies, social science, agriculture and veterinary medicine would be in UCD alone; the faculties of dentistry and pharmacy would be in TCD alone; statutory provision was to be made for the recognition of theology (divinity) as a university disci-pline

- the College of Education for Teachers of Specialist Subjects and the National College of Physical Education, both in Limerick, were to have a joint Governing Body of twenty-five members and become a recog-nised college of the NUI
- the Governing Bodies of UCD, TCD, UCC, UCG, Maynooth, NIHE Dublin and NIHE Limerick were each to consist of twenty-five mem-bers
- University Senates would consist of thirty-five members.

Outcome of the Burke proposals

The Burke proposals were a cause of much concern in the Irish university sector and particularly in TCD and UCD, in respect of which decisions were announced in relation to the distribution of their faculties and other issues. There were other proposals relating to altering the sizes of their Governing Bodies that in turn raised the possibility of legislative changes and the imposition of increased state control over their operations.

The reaction of senior staff in the universities was summarised by F. S. Lyons, Provost of TCD, in January 1976:

> Most of us during the past year have tried repeatedly to work through the various problems presented by the Minister for Education's state-ment of December 1974. There are so many unknown factors in the situation that to achieve a balanced analysis is well nigh impossible and it is not in the least surprising that feelings of anger and frustra-tion have sometimes boiled over.[12]

Following considerable representation and lobbying, many of the Burke proposals, like the O'Malley proposals before them, were never imple-mented; some were partly implemented and only a small number were fully implemented. In general those relating to the universities were not implemented, apart from those concerned with dentistry, pharmacy, agri-

---

12. Lyons, F S, *The Technology Tangle in Dublin* (Dublin: Society of College Lectur-ers), 1976.

culture and veterinary medicine. No conjoint board to co-ordinate the Dublin universities was established and the Conference of Heads of Irish Universities (CHIU) was the closest to a Conference of Irish Universities to be set up. On the other side of the binary divide, however, the proposals relating to the NIHEs and RTCs were broadly carried through and the NCEA was the closest approximation achieved to the proposed Council for Technological Education.

NATIONAL INSTITUTES OF HIGHER EDUCATION ACTS 1980

The National Institute of Higher Education (Limerick) Act 1980, removed that Institute from the NUI and brought it under the aegis of the NCEA, to which degree awarding power had been restored in 1977.[13] In fact, two identical Acts were passed in 1980 to place the two NIHEs, in Limerick and Dublin, on a statutory footing. These Acts defined the functions of the NIHEs in relation to academic quality, standards and levels of programmes, as providing primary degree, diploma and certificate as well as postgraduate level courses, and engaging in research work. The NIHEs were not given any awarding power but were thereafter accredited by the NCEA and their graduates received NCEA degrees.

The Academic Council of each NIHE was empowered to:

• offer appropriate programmes of study

• establish structures to implement them

• develop research

• put academic regulations in place

• conduct examinations

• evaluate academic progress of students

• organise tutorial and other academic counselling for students.

Issues relating to the assurance of quality were not explicitly addressed in these Acts. By 1986 the role of the NCEA in relation to quality assurance in the NIHEs involved the approval of courses based on an institutional self-evaluation and the participation of university and industry/business specialists from Ireland and abroad in curriculum development and Boards of Studies. The NCEA also appointed external examiners from nomina-

---

13. *National Institute of Higher Education (Limerick) Act* and *National Institute of Higher Education (Dublin) Act* (Baile Átha Cliath: Oifig an tSoláthair), 1980.

tions of academic and business experts submitted by the institutions. Arrangements for the admission of students were devolved to the institutions themselves, subject to government policies and regulations set out by the CAO.

GREEN PAPER ON EDUCATION 1985

In 1985, the Minister for Education, Gemma Hussey TD, issued a Green Paper on education which, among other issues, considered the place of the DIT in the higher education system.[14] The general thrust of this discussion document was a far-reaching proposal for the reform of the system of Vocational Education Committees (VECs) into a fewer number of Local Education Committees (LECs). These LECs would cater for all second-level schools in the regions. These proposal would have reduced the long established binary divide in second level education between the vocational system and the voluntary secondary school system. Indeed, by that time considerable momentum had developed behind the establishment of a new comprehensive type of second level school — the community school or community college — and this has been the pattern since then.

Because the DIT and the RTCs were under the aegis of the VECs, the question of whether these institutions would transfer to the new LECs was considered. In relation to the DIT, the green paper proposed that it be established on a statutory basis. It was envisaged that this statutory base might provide for a Governing Body or Board of Management (containing strong representation from the CDVEC) and an Academic Council appointed by Governing Body to assist it in "planning, co-ordination, development and overseeing" the educational programmes of the Institute. The document discussed the possibility of designating the DIT under the HEA, particularly in the light of its experience under the partnership with the University of Dublin and its different character in quantitative and qualitative terms from that of the RTCs. The long association of the Institute with the CDVEC and the amount of apprentice work within the Institute were adduced as possible arguments against designation under the HEA. The Green Paper envisaged a director for the Institute and six heads of colleges (or schools) responsible to the director.

In the event, the reform of the VEC system was never implemented,

---

14. *Partners in Education: Serving Community Needs* (Baile Átha Cliath: Oifig an tSoláthair), 1985.

but the recommendations in respect of the DIT eventually found partial expression in the Dublin Institute of Technology Act 1992 (see Chapter 5).

INTERNATIONAL STUDY GROUP ON TECHNOLOGICAL EDUCATION 1986–1987

The two NIHEs in Limerick and Dublin sought to improve their status by persuading the Minister for Education in 1986 to establish an International Study Group to examine technological education outside the universities and advise on the case for a new technological university.[15] The work of this group can now be recognised as broadly touching on quality audit and accreditation of higher education in general, and of these two institutions (NIHE Limerick and NIHE Dublin) in particular. This was the first occasion that such a process had been undertaken within the state. The International Study Group comprised the following members.

Members of the International Study Group on Technological Education 1986–1987

Chairman:
Dr T. P. Hardiman, Chairman, Investment Bank of Ireland

Deputy Chairman:
Professor M. J. MacCormac, Professor of Business Administration (Emeritus), University College, Dublin

Membership:
Dr R. E. D. Bishop, Vice-Chancellor, Brunel University, England
Dr O. H. G. Mahrenholtz, Technische Universität Hamburg and Vice-President, Deutsche Forschungsgemeinschaft, West Germany
Dr D. T. Wright, President, University of Waterloo, Canada

Secretary:
M. Gleeson, Higher Education Authority

In its report, the study group considered management, planning, standards and quality assurance matters to be of significance. It concluded that in respect of technological education, the "existing universities serve the country well, and will continue to play a central role in technological education in Ireland". It recommended that the HEA "should be fully involved

---

15. *Technological Education, Report of the International Study Group to the Minister for Education* (Baile Átha Cliath: Oifig an tSoláthair), 1987.

in all matters relating to the planning, financing and co-ordination of all third-level activities". In relation to the NIHEs it was the Group's view that their standards of scholarship were as high as those of the universities, that they should be given the title and status of self-accrediting universities, and that their legislation should be amended to "give them degree awarding powers and to provide statutory Academic Councils with responsibility" for their academic affairs.

The report also recommended that the DIT and the RTCs be established on a statutory basis with their funding coming through the HEA. It suggested these measures would give these institutions increased autonomy and allow them to engage in research, development and consultancy services for external organisations.

University of Limerick and Dublin City University Acts 1989

The report of the International Study Group specifically recommended that the NIHEs in Limerick and Dublin should be established as universities, with the NIHE Limerick having the title of University of Limerick and the NIHE Dublin having the title Dublin City University or the University of Leinster. The report further recommended that the title "Technological University" should not be used because of the broader nature of the activities in the two institutions proposed as universities. Acts of the Oireachtas were enacted in 1989 conferring university status on the University of Limerick and Dublin City University.

The effect of these Acts was the transfer of the former NIHEs across the binary divide in higher education from the technological side to the universities' side. This transfer was achieved with remarkably little public discussion or worry about academic drift or the effect of the transfer on the rest of the technological sector.

Green Paper on Education 1992

Public debate on higher education in Ireland was stimulated with the publication by the Minister for Education, Séamus Brennan TD, of a comprehensive Green Paper on education in 1992.[16] This Green Paper indicated many areas for legitimate questioning in relation to quality in higher education, "the concern and care for the students and the ways in which this is

---

16. *Education for a Changing World* (Baile Átha Cliath: Oifig an tSoláthair), 1992.

demonstrated in the institution; the quality of teaching and support provided by staff; the percentage of new entrants who proceed to graduation;
the output and quality of research; the efficient use of resources and the
procedures in place in institutions to review quality continually". It saw
as key the provision of appropriate staff development and, in consequence,
the improvement of the quality of teaching, guidance and assistance available to students.

The Green Paper addressed a number of other aspects of quality assurance. It suggested that the university institutions should have maximum
flexibility in developing courses, but that within policy, budgetary and
physical resource constraints, courses should be run cost-efficiently and
not adversely affect other courses.

In relation to the DIT and the RTCs, the Green Paper suggested that an
appropriate balance between certificate, diploma and degree graduates be
maintained, and that the value of certificate and diploma awards as termi-
nal qualifications should not be undermined. It advised that any degree
courses developed in these institutions should not be such as to be able to
be offered more cost-effectively by a university and should be aimed at a
proven industrial need based on effective liaison with and support from
industry. It suggested that the NCEA would approve the programmes and
report annually to the Department of Education on the national and local
patterns of course development. The Green Paper also recommended that
the NCEA undertake a review of entry standards to courses in the DIT and
the RTCs, together with the success and progression records of their students. This review was envisaged as being linked to a review of standards
of achievement in each of the colleges.

This Green Paper was the first policy document from the Department
of Education acknowledging the dual or binary system of higher education provision in Ireland, and the official concern to provide some overall
co-ordination between the two sectors in the system.

DUBLIN INSTITUTE OF TECHNOLOGY ACT 1992

Following the recommendations in the Green Paper on education in 1985
and the report of the International Study Group on Technological Education in 1987, the Dublin Institute of Technology Act 1992 established DIT
as an autonomous institution, largely independent of the CDVEC, under
which its constituent colleges had previously operated. (This Act, its context and terms are discussed in some detail in Chapter 5.) Among other
things, the Act set out as the functions of the Institute the provision of

vocational and technical education and training for the economic, technological, scientific, commercial, industrial, social and cultural development of the State. It gave the Institute the authority to grant diplomas, certificates and other educational awards, excluding degrees. The Act also empowered the Institute to engage in research, consultancy and development work. In 1997, after a review in 1995/1996 of the Institute's quality assurance procedures by an international review team on behalf of the Minister for Education (see Chapter 11), an order was made under the Act assigning to the DIT the function of awarding primary and postgraduate degrees and honorary awards.

The Academic Council of the DIT was entrusted by the Act with academic powers to offer appropriate programmes of study and establish structures to implement them. It was also empowered to engage in research and development, select, admit, retain or exclude students, put academic regulations in place, conduct examinations and evaluate academic progress of students. It could appoint external examiners and organise tutorial and other academic counselling for students.

REGIONAL TECHNICAL COLLEGES ACT 1992

In general, the Dublin Institute of Technology Act and the Regional Technical Colleges Act 1992 had much in common, both having the same general structure and identical wording in several sections. Indeed the Bills for both Acts were introduced to the Dáil simultaneously but subsequently they were debated separately, particularly in relation to amendments that were introduced.

One of the special features of the DIT legislation was that it gave to the Institute the power to confer its own academic awards, unlike the RTC legislation that did not have such a provision. There were also significant differences relating to the functions given to the respective Academic Councils. In the DIT legislation additional provisions empowered the Academic Council to appoint external examiners and confer honorary awards. The additional functions given to the DIT and its Academic Council were consistent with the DIT making its own awards, whereas the RTCs did not have authority to confer their own awards. In the late 1990s some of the RTCs, by then renamed Institutes of Technology, were granted the power to make certificate and diploma awards.

STEERING COMMITTEE ON THE FUTURE DEVELOPMENT OF HIGHER EDUCATION 1993–1995

In December 1993, the Minister for Education, Niamh Bhreathnach TD, requested the HEA to establish a Steering Committee to advise her on the future development of the higher education sector. The committee was broadly representative of the higher education institutions, the social partners, government departments and other interested organisations. The committee was supported by a technical working group that reported on future growth and its distribution between the university and non-university sectors, the financial implications of the growth projected, the geographic distribution of higher education need and provision, and the measures needed to facilitate participation by disadvantaged, mature and second-chance students.[17]

In many ways the work of the Steering Committee was a preparation for the relevant sections of the White Paper on education (see below), which was issued before the report of the committee.[18] The report of the Steering Committee emphasised a range of key considerations in higher education, including:

- quality assurance
- co-ordination across higher education institutions
- equity and equality in the system
- adult and further education
- the role of higher education in economic development
- the growing cost of higher education.

The report made projections of the likely growth in higher education in two phases, the first until 2000 and then from 2000 to 2015. It suggested that there would be substantial growth in numbers of part-time and mature or second-chance students in the near future. The report endorsed the "institutional diversity" or binary structure of higher education comprising the two distinctive sectors — the university and non-university sectors — to meet the varying needs of students, society and the economy, while seeking co-ordination between the two strands. It projected the establishment of Teastas (see below) to help structure quality in further and higher

---

17. *Interim Report of the Steering Committee's Technical Working Group* (Dublin: Higher Education Authority), 1995.
18. *Report of the Steering Committee on the Future Development of Higher Education* (Dublin: Higher Education Authority), 1995.

education. It noted the more applied nature of the courses and modes of delivery in the non-university sector when compared with the more academic approach in the universities. The report first recommended that the title of Regional Technical College be changed to Regional Institute of Technology to reflect the changing role of these colleges. The report recommended a further detailed study of the balance of programme provision in both the university and non-university sectors.

WHITE PAPER ON EDUCATION 1995

The government's comprehensive White Paper on education, published in April 1995 by the Minister for Education, Niamh Bhreathnach TD, set out the background and policy framework against which future developments in Irish education, including higher education, would be progressed.[19] The White Paper identified the following as the considerations, most of them brought forward from the Green Paper of 1992, that would underpin the approach to be pursued in relation to higher education:

- the promotion of equality in and through higher education
- the recognition of the legitimate autonomy of institutions, particularly in relation to determining the educational aims and content of programmes
- the promotion of the highest standards of quality
- the preservation of diversity and balance of provision, within the system, while avoiding unnecessary overlap or duplication
- the promotion and facilitation of the key leadership role of higher education as a source of social and economic development, together with the need to ensure continuing relevance to the needs of the economy and the promotion of links between institutions and their social and economic environments
- the continuous development of a framework of accountability for individual institutions and for the higher education system as a whole
- the provision of an appropriate legislative framework, which affirms well-established values while reflecting the role of higher education in modern society.

The White Paper proposed that "system differentiation" between the uni-

19. *Charting our Education Future* (Baile Átha Cliath: Oifig an tSoláthair), 1995.

versities and the so-called technological institutions or non-university in-stitutions — the binary system — should be maintained. It stated that "diversity of institutions and the separate missions of the two broad sec-tors will be maintained to ensure maximum flexibility and responsiveness to the needs of students and the wide variety of social and economic re-quirements". It had been pointed out in the 1992 Green Paper on educa-tion that while the HEA had been established to have a broad advisory role in relation to the entire higher education sector, its activities had re-lated largely to the universities alone. The White Paper proposed that the HEA would fund all the higher education institutions — the DIT and the RTCs, as well as the universities.

However the White Paper acknowledged the particular position and status of the DIT, "given its historical development, size and present aca-demic profile". It looked to the completion of the work in the DIT, of creating a "single unified Institute, including the establishment of appro-priate academic and administrative structures". It projected a balance of programmes in the Institute with more degree courses than in the RTCs, but still having a "substantial level of provision at certificate and diploma level". In relation to research it saw the RTCs being engaged in "regionally oriented applied research" while special, but unspecified, considerations would apply to the DIT. The White Paper thus described the particularity of the DIT as straddling the divide in the binary system, between the RTCs on one side and the universities on the other.

UNIVERSITIES ACT 1997

The Universities Act 1997 had a number of aims and aspects relating to drawing all the universities in the Republic of Ireland into broadly stand-ard structures and internal regulatory frameworks. It was the first piece of academic legislation to specifically set out the responsibilities of the in-stitutions for academic quality assurance. The Act set out terms and con-ditions for the autonomy of the institutions. It also reached deeply into the governance of universities.

Under this legislation, among the functions elaborated for a university and underpinning its autonomy were:

• the maintenance, management and administration of the property, money, assets and rights of the university

• acquisition and disposal of land or other property

• acceptance of gifts of money, land or other property.

The university had "the right and responsibility to preserve and promote the traditional principles of academic freedom in the conduct of its internal and external affairs". It was entitled to regulate its affairs in accordance with its independent ethos and traditions and the traditional principles of academic freedom, but under the limitations of being duty bound to promote and preserve equality of opportunity and access, using resources effectively and efficiently, and being publicly accountable. At the level of the individual member of academic staff, he or she was free, "within the law, in her/his teaching, research and any other activities in or outside the university, to question and test received wisdom, to put forward new ideas and to state controversial or unpopular opinions and (should) not be disadvantaged, or subject to less favourable treatment by the university, for the exercise of that freedom".

In relation to academic quality assurance, one of the objects of a university was specified as promoting "the highest standards in, and quality of, teaching and research". In regard to staff recruitment, the Act empowered the university to develop transparent interview and other procedures to ensure participation of high quality candidates in the recruitment process, and thereby recruit high quality academic staff. The Act also extended the ideas of quality in a social direction, requiring the university to "have regard to the attainment of gender balance and equality of opportunity among the students and employees of the university" and to "promote access to the university and to university education by economically or socially disadvantaged people and by people from sections of society significantly under-represented in the student body".

Each university was to have an academic council that would have the responsibility to design and develop programmes of study, establish structures to implement those, develop research, and manage the selection, admission, retention and exclusion of students. It was to develop statutes to regulate the academic affairs of the university, including the conduct of examinations, the determination of examination results, the establishment of procedures for appeals by students relating to the results of such examinations and the evaluation of academic progress. Furthermore it was to recommend the awarding of fellowships, scholarships, bursaries, prizes or other awards, and arrange tutorial or other academic counselling for students.

In a new departure for universities in Ireland, the legislation required each university to prepare a strategic development plan, setting out the aims of the university for its operation and development, including its strategy for achieving these aims, and for carrying out the functions of the university during a period of three years or more. This would enable each university to be examined in respect of its strategic plan and audited in relation to its achievement of this plan.

The Act specifically required each university to "establish procedures for quality assurance aimed at improving the quality of education and related services provided by the university". These procedures were to include the evaluation, at regular intervals, of each department and faculty of the university, and any service provided by the university, by employees of the university in the first instance (a self-study), the assessment by those, including students, availing of the teaching, research and other services provided by the university (part of the self-study), and the evaluation by persons, other than employees, who are competent to make national and international comparisons on the quality of teaching and research and the provision of other services at university level (an external audit). The findings of such evaluation and assessment were to be published. The university was to be required to implement any findings arising out of such an evaluation carried out, unless, having regard to the resources available to the university or for other reasons, it would be impractical or unreasonable to do so. Furthermore the university must periodically review the effectiveness of these internal evaluation and external assessment procedures as well as the implementation of the findings arising out of them.

The university legislation introduced another possible element of external audit in the university Visitor, who could be asked by the Minister for Education and Science to inquire into the academic or other affairs of a university if there were reasonable grounds for considering that the functions of that university were being performed in a manner that might be in breach of the regulations of the university.

The Act effected a number of significant changes in the role of the HEA in relation to the higher education institutions designated to its remit, particularly in relation to academic quality assurance matters. For instance it required the HEA to review the strategic development plan of each institution, monitor the implementation of the plan and publish a report on such review and monitoring. The HEA was also to review and report on the procedures established by each university for evaluating the quality of its teaching and research. Significantly, under this legislation, the HEA was entrusted with monitoring and publishing reports on the implementation of the institution's policies on equality and access. The HEA was given a further role in setting the staffing levels and relative priorities between different activities in a university, in that it might issue guidelines on the numbers and grades of employees in the university and also the part of the budget to be applied to the different activities of the university. The HEA might also place restrictions and conditions on the use of moneys it distributed to a university.

The Universities Act decreed that an institution might not use the title "university" unless it had been designated as a university under the Act. The Act also included in Section 9 procedures, to be administered by the HEA, by which an institution might be evaluated in order to be designated as a university.

QUALIFICATIONS (EDUCATION AND TRAINING) ACT 1999

As proposed in the government's White Paper on education in 1995, the Minister for Education established Teastas, the Irish National Certification Authority, in September 1995 on a preparatory basis with an interim board. In relation to higher education, the authority was to have the following responsibilities:

- developing, implementing, regulating and supervising the certification of all non-university programmes
- elaborating the plans, programmes and budgets necessary for achieving these functions
- establishing, directing, supervising and regulating a national qualification framework
- being the national agency for ensuring international recognition for all qualifications under its aegis.[20]

In furtherance of the plans for Teastas, the Qualifications (Education and Training) Act 1999 projected the establishment of a National Qualifications Authority. The objects of the Authority will be:

- to establish and maintain a "framework of qualifications for the development, recognition and award of qualifications in the State, based on standards of knowledge, skill or competence"
- to establish, promote and maintain the standards of awards of the new Further Education and Training Awards Council, the new Higher Education and Training Awards Council, the DIT and any university established under Section 9 of the Universities Act 1997
- to promote and facilitate access, transfer and progression within this framework.

---

20. *First Report* (Dublin: Teastas), 1997.

In general the existing universities are not to come under the aegis of the Authority.

The Act outlined procedures for the validation of a programme leading to an award and the quality assurance of such a programme. In relation to the DIT for instance, the Authority will require the Institute to establish quality assurance and enhancement procedures. These procedures will include "regular evaluation of programmes, evaluation by learners, evaluation of related services and publication of findings arising out of the application of these procedures". Furthermore the Authority may make "binding recommendations" to the Institute, arising from these procedures. It will also be entitled to review the effectiveness of the procedures and the implementation of recommendations arising from them. It is of some significance that these and other provisions of the Act enact amendments to the Dublin Institute of Technology Act 1992.

The Act also made some amendments to the Universities Act 1997 and even the Higher Education Authority Act 1971. In relation to quality assurance matters provided for in the Universities Act, the HEA was to consult with the National Qualifications Authority in advising the universities. A Section 9 university (one established under Section 9 of the Universities Act) would submit its strategic plan to the Authority for approval, a provision not envisaged in the Universities Act. Also a Section 9 university would not be governed by the quality assurance sections of the Universities Act but rather by the procedures of this new Act.

The two new Councils — the Further Education and Training Awards Council and the Higher Education and Training Awards Council — were also to be established by this legislation. The latter in particular would subsume the structure and functions of the NCEA, which this legislation would dissolve.

However, the proposed national framework of qualifications will be relatively limited in that it will include the universities only peripherally. For instance while the Act looked to the National Qualification Authority to "ensure" the DIT and Section 9 universities implement procedures determined by the Authority in relation to access, transfer and progression, it would only advise existing universities on implementing such procedures. Postgraduate research activities, academic/industrial collaboration, and consultancy work received no attention in the Act, even though they have considerable impact on taught courses at all levels.

The Act acknowledged a distinction between the DIT and the regional Institutes of Technology (ITs) founded under the Regional Technical Colleges Act 1992. The latter would be subject to the controls of the two Councils, particularly the Higher Education and Training Council which would make the awards for the majority of the ITs. The Act also made a distinction between the DIT and any future Section 9 university on the one hand and the existing universities on the other hand. In another broad sense it established a clear distinction between the existing universities, which were largely excluded from its remit, and the DIT and the other ITs, the so-called technological sector, which were encompassed by the Act.

This Act therefore copper-fastened the binary system of higher education in Ireland despite evidence of official concern expressed in the Green Paper. This is in contrast with the situation in the second level system where the binary divide has long been discredited as socially divisive and was eventually abandoned over a decade ago. The binary system has been socially divisive in higher education as well. The way in which it has shaped — and possibly misshaped — Ireland's democracy needs further research. It will be important to monitor how it contributes to the social structure in the decades ahead and how the national qualifications framework may help to mollify the sharper edges of the social stratification that it can foster.

SUMMARY

The expansion of higher education begun in the 1960s, gathered pace in the 1970s and was manifested through new statutory structures and new institutions.

The reform and restructuring of Irish higher education begun in the 1970s, carried into the 1980s and continued at a greatly accelerated pace in the 1990s.

The 1990s were a decade of extensive development of public policy and legislation relating to higher education in Ireland. At the same time, the system continued to expand to meet the needs of Irish society and industry. In this respect the highlight of the decade for the DIT was the passing of the Dublin Institute of Technology Act 1992, which established the Institute on a statutory footing and made it substantially independent of its former parent body, the CDVEC. The Universities Act 1997 also affected the development of the Institute, and at the end of the decade the new Qualifications (Education and Training) Act 1999, to establish the national qualifications framework and determine some key boundary conditions within which the Institute will function in the future, has further implications.

Chapter 4

Partnership Agreement between the CDVEC/DIT and the University of Dublin (1976–present)

Among the elements of the Burke proposals, outlined in Chapter 3, was one that promised no capital investment in the engineering science area in the University of Dublin. This alarmed the university. The relative isolation of the university from general Irish society, highlighted in the 1967 report of the Commission on Higher Education, and its political weakness and vulnerability to the Burke proposals, probably added to this alarm.[1] These factors and the element in the Burke proposals indicating that the National Institute of Higher Education (NIHE) in Dublin might become a recognised college or constituent college of one of the Dublin universities, coupled with the general understanding that the NIHE would be the implementation of the Ballymun Project of the City of Dublin Vocational Education Committee (CDVEC), all formed the background and facilitated the urgent discussions on co-operation that began between the CDVEC and the University of Dublin in early 1975.

BACKGROUND TO THE PARTNERSHIP AGREEMENT BETWEEN THE CDVEC/DIT AND THE UNIVERSITY OF DUBLIN

A substantial area of common interest had developed between the University of Dublin and the CDVEC colleges. There had been already considerable contact between the two parties, e.g. the sharing of laboratory resources and staff between the university and the engineering departments at the Colleges of Technology in Bolton Street and Kevin Street. In the words of F. S. Lyons, Provost of TCD, in 1976,

> Our long previous experience of friendly relations between our En-

---

1. Commission on Higher Education 1960–1967, *I. Presentation and Summary of Report, op. cit.*

gineering School and their opposite numbers in Bolton Street and Kevin Street suggests that in teaching and research, in the sharing of facilities and of people, there is valuable common ground.

By that time some fifty engineering diploma graduates from the Bolton Street and Kevin Street colleges had been admitted to postgraduate engineering courses of TCD and had successfully graduated with master's degrees. Some of them were continuing their studies to doctoral level. They had shown by their performance on these courses that their academic standards were at least comparable with those of graduates of Irish university engineering schools. This confirmed a decision already taken by the Institution of Engineers of Ireland and some of the British engineering institutions to accredit the Bolton Street and Kevin Street courses as meeting in full their academic requirements for corporate membership. Some members of academic staff from each of the colleges had contributed to the TCD postgraduate courses, acting as lecturers and tutors, and some elements of these postgraduate courses had been conducted in the Bolton Street and Kevin Street colleges.

In the light of the Minister's announcement that degree awards in the NIHEs in the immediate future would be provided by the Irish universities, informal discussions between representatives of the university and the CDVEC colleges led to a proposal that the award of the University of Dublin (Trinity College Dublin, TCD) degrees be made to engineering diploma holders, the standard of which was already familiar to TCD. This proposal was given added urgency when the UK based Institution of Electrical Engineers announced about that time that in future the normal academic requirement for corporate membership would be an engineering degree award which in turn would adversely affect the position of the Kevin Street college diploma graduates who aspired to membership of that institution.

In May 1975, following a formal accreditation visit by TCD representatives to the Bolton Street and Kevin Street colleges and a review of their engineering courses, a proposal was presented to the university's Council for the award of BSc (Eng) degrees with honours classification to those successful in the final Diploma in Engineering examinations in 1975. The approval was given on an *ad hoc* basis pending the development of a more formal arrangement as part of what was to become a longer-term relationship between the two institutions.

There were other courses in the CDVEC colleges which already enjoyed recognition from the appropriate professional bodies as meeting in full the academic requirements for corporate membership or were otherwise recognised as being of honours degree standard. Rather than proceeding on a course by course basis, it was agreed that it would be more prudent to develop an overall operational framework between both institutions for processing any courses that the CDVEC would propose as appropriate for degree awards of the university. This led to the partnership agreement between the university and the CDVEC that was formalised in April 1976 and has provided the basis for the ongoing relationship between the two institutions since then.[2]

IMPLEMENTATION OF THE PARTNERSHIP AGREEMENT

The partnership agreement formalised the relationship between the university and CDVEC and in particular the third level colleges under its aegis. It established the underlying principle of equal partnership, parity of esteem and respect for the separate autonomy, identity and ethos of each partner. The formal recognition of the CDVEC colleges as "recognised colleges" was considered to be inappropriate, because this would have involved a degree of control over the CDVEC colleges and a client status for the colleges that would not provide a suitable basis for the absolute parity which was to be the cornerstone of the partnership. While it would be appropriate for the degree level courses in the colleges, it might undermine the important non-degree courses. Also it was felt that a partnership based on close personal contacts in the different discipline areas would be likely to lead to the development of a better relationship in the longer term.

In October 1976, the Liaison Council representing the two institutions approved two key policy documents which set out the framework and operational procedures under which the agreement was intended to function. The first of these was the Guideline in Relation to the Award of Degrees.[3]

In this framework the CDVEC colleges would continue to maintain control over all matters pertaining to the administration and conduct of its courses, namely:

• the admission of their students

---

2. University of Dublin/City of Dublin Vocational Education Committee, *Agreement between the City of Dublin Vocational Education Committee and the University of Dublin* (Dublin), April 1976.
3. University of Dublin/City of Dublin Vocational Education Committee Liaison Council, *Guideline in Relation to the Award of Degrees* (Dublin), October 1976.

- the conduct of the courses and the assessment of their students
- the academic standards of the courses
- the nomination and appointment of external examiners, in consultation with the university.

It was acknowledged by the CDVEC that the university equally had a concern for the academic standards of the courses concerned and of the graduates eligible for its degree awards. In consequence, provision was made for the university to have the right of access on request to information about the operation or other aspects of the courses that were involved.

Forms of co-operation envisaged

The range of forms of co-operation envisaged in the partnership agreement included sharing of staff and facilities, co-operation in course design and operation, promoting the mobility of students and staff, co-operation in research and consultation on more general matters. The initial assessment of each course by the university, together with the joint approval of external examiners, provided the university with a means of satisfying itself as to the academic standards of the courses. External examiners drawn from senior levels in academic and/or professional practice reported to both the university and the appropriate college in the CDVEC/DIT. The DIT's system of five-yearly course reviews allowed for participation by the university, thereby providing it with further and continuing assurances in respect of quality, standards and the operation of the courses on an ongoing basis.

DEVELOPMENT OF PROGRAMMES UNDER THE PARTNERSHIP AGREEMENT

The second key policy document agreed by the Liaison Council in October 1976 was the Procedural Guidelines for Inter-Colleges Committees.[4]

As a development of the *ad hoc* arrangements for the engineering courses under the procedures for the operation of the agreement, *prima facie* cases were established in 1976 for existing DIT diploma courses in architecture, construction economics and environmental economics and a new option in structural engineering. After full evaluations, graduates of these courses became eligible for degree awards of the university. In the

---

4.   University of Dublin/City of Dublin Vocational Education Committee Liaison Council, *Procedural Guidelines for Inter-Colleges Committees* (Dublin), October 1976.

same year similar degree recognition was accorded, following similar evaluations, in respect of the diploma courses in applied sciences (Kevin Street), business studies (Rathmines), marketing techniques (Mountjoy Square), and hotel and catering management (Cathal Brugha Street).

Other CDVEC/DIT diploma courses subsequently recognised by the university for degree awards were:

• human nutrition and dietetics, Kevin Street (1982) (a joint course)

• building services, Bolton Street (1983)

• environmental health, Cathal Brugha Street (1984)

• music education, College of Music (1985) (a joint course, which also involves the Royal Irish Academy of Music).

Still more recently the processes were completed for the recognition of diploma courses in biomedical sciences (1990) in Kevin Street, management law (1990), communications (film and broadcasting) (1992), communications (journalism) (1995), management services (1994) and health services management (1996) in Aungier Street, music performance (1991) in Adelaide Road, and administration and marketing (1995) in Mountjoy Square. Additional options have been introduced in the Kevin Street applied sciences and engineering courses and approved during the five-yearly reviews.

A full listing of the DIT courses which were approved by the university under the terms of the partnership agreement is given in Table 8.1.

The development of each of these honours degree courses across the Institute was predicated on many years of conducting successful certificate and diploma courses in related topics. Such courses served to test the market and to develop the competencies of staff, so that the emergence of degree level courses was an organic process.

Table 8.2 shows the numbers of graduates classified by discipline area who having received DIT diploma awards also became eligible for appropriate degree awards of the university. In 1975, a total of twenty-eight engineering graduates from Bolton Street and Kevin Street became eligible for degree awards. In 1999, the number of graduates eligible for degree awards was 946. Since the inception of the partnership agreement in 1975, 11,965 graduates of DIT diploma courses have become eligible for degree awards of the university.

In keeping with the terms of the partnership agreement, external examiners, agreed by both the DIT and the university, have played an important role in underwriting the standards of the degrees awarded. Normally, at least two such examiners with expertise appropriate to the discipline

**Arnold Graves (1847–1930), founder of the technical school system
in Dublin**

The old Kevin Street College (replaced in the 1960s)

Kevin Street College

Chatham Row College

Rathmines College

Mountjoy Square College

Bolton Street College

Cathal Brugha Street College

A rear view of Aungier Street College

The first Directorate of the DIT, from left, Robert Lawlor, Frank Heneghan, Michael O'Donnell (Acting President), Frank Brennan and James Hickey

The Directorate of the DIT from 1996–2000 at back, from left, John Ratcliffe, David Gillingham, Paul O'Sullivan, Ray Wills, Matt Hussey, Declan Glynn, Michael Mulvey; at front, from left, Frank Brennan, Brendan Goldsmith (President), Ellen Hazelkorn, Robert Lawlor

are appointed, with one drawn from an appropriate academic institution at home or abroad and the other from industry or professional practice. In accordance with their terms of appointment they report to both the DIT and the University of Dublin.

The DIT procedures of rigorous course validation and ongoing five-yearly reviews, in both of which the university is involved, are quality assurance arrangements that compare favourably with those pertaining in any other institutions in Ireland. They ensure that the standards of the courses leading to the degree awards are maintained to the satisfaction of both partners.

INTER-COLLEGES COMMITTEES

Under the partnership agreement, inter-colleges committees were established relating to the different course disciplines as indicated in Table 4.1 and a joint co-ordinating committee was set up for the joint course in human nutrition and dietetics. These committees embody the efforts to develop close personal relationships between staff members in the two institutions, particularly those in related disciplines. They are responsible to the Liaison Council and their role involves the monitoring, co-ordinating and reviewing of particular areas of co-operation, and giving advice where considered appropriate, having regard to the provisions of the partnership agreement.

DEVELOPMENT OF POSTGRADUATE PROGRAMMES

The partnership agreement with the University of Dublin has helped to stimulate increasing postgraduate research activity within the DIT. As a logical part of the development of the agreement, interest and commitment among DIT staff and graduates in pursuing higher degree awards through both research and taught programmes underwent considerable growth.

A fee-waiver (zero fee) scheme was introduced in the late 1970s to facilitate DIT academic staff engaging in research activity to obtain a higher degree of the university. Through this scheme the university contributed significantly to DIT staff development as well as to the growth of its research programmes. It has also been a catalyst for co-operative research projects in some discipline areas. More than sixty DIT staff have participated in the scheme since it was initiated and have been conferred with

Table 4.1: Inter-Colleges/Joint Co-ordinating Committees

Architecture	relating to Architecture BSc(Arch), Property Economics and Construction Economics BSc(Surv) (Bolton Street)
Engineering	relating to Electrical/Electronic Engineering BSc(Eng) (Kevin Street) and Mechanical, Manufacturing, Building Services and Structural Engineering BSc(Eng) (Bolton Street)
Applied Sciences	relating to Biological Science, Chemistry, Computing, Mathematics and Physics BSc(AppSc) (Kevin Street)
Management	relating to Hotel and Catering Management BSc(Mgmt) (Cathal Brugha Street), Marketing and Administration BSc(Mgmt)(Mountjoy Square) and Business Studies, Management Law, Management Services, Health Services Management BSc(Mgmt) and Communications BSc(Media) (Aungier Street)
Environmental Health	relating to Environmental Health BSc(EnvH) (Cathal Brugha Street)
Medical Laboratory Science	relating to Biomedical Science BSc(AppSc) (Kevin Street)
Human Nutrition and Dietetics	relating to a joint degree for this discipline BSc(HN&D) (Joint Co-ordinating Committee)
Postgraduate Studies	relating to postgraduate research

higher degrees. The DIT has also provided funding for additional places on the scheme in response to growing demand.

Proposals for the extension of the provisions of the partnership agreement to cater for postgraduate activities in the DIT were frequently raised at meetings of the Liaison Council and inter-colleges committees. However, it was not until the late 1980s that these proposals were more formally addressed. The Liaison Council established a joint committee representing both partners in 1988, "to provide orderly arrangements for the considerable amount of research activity already taking place". This joint committee prepared a memorandum that addressed both postgraduate taught programmes and postgraduate research activities. In June 1989 the Liaison Council adopted the proposals as set out in the memorandum. However, some difficulties arose later in implementing the memorandum in relation to postgraduate studies by research, partly due to the absence of suitable structures within the DIT and partly due to a reluctance by some departments in TCD to become more involved and co-operate with the DIT in this activity. In 1992 these issues were addressed and a further memorandum of understanding "concerning the registration of DIT candidates for higher degrees by research" was agreed between the University of Dublin and the DIT, dealing with the registration, supervision, progression and examination of DIT postgraduate students pursuing higher degrees in TCD. It also provided for a remission of up to 50 per cent of fees paid to the university where the work was wholly carried out in the DIT.

In addition, at an informal level, a limited amount of collaboration has taken place in relation to staff exchange, exchange of equipment and shared use of facilities and joint research.

DIT/TCD joint research seed funding scheme

A joint research seed funding scheme was initiated in 1995, funded from the Institute's and the university's resources. It was aimed at assisting staff members in the two institutions to develop joint research projects, which might lead to European or other external funds. In assisting over twenty projects since its inception, this scheme has helped to develop a number of inter-institution research collaborations.

A call is issued for this programme once each year, internally within the DIT and TCD, and the selection process is carried out by a joint committee of senior staff from the two institutions.

REVIEWS OF THE PARTNERSHIP AGREEMENT IN THE 1980S

TCD review 1987–1988

In 1987 the Council of the university established a committee to undertake a review of the partnership and to consider whether the best interests of TCD would be served by continuing or changing the arrangements in the partnership agreement. The review committee used a questionnaire to survey the members of TCD staff who were involved in the arrangements and also received a brief statement from each.

The report of the review committee summarised the remarks received thus:

- the lack of research in the DIT adversely affected the quality of teaching at honours level
- the attendance of TCD representatives at examination boards was of a formal character and did not allow an opportunity to judge standards
- the various inter-colleges committees tended to be unsatisfactory in composition and function and did not exercise supervision over the relevant courses
- the links between TCD and the DIT were administrative rather than academic in character
- the DIT staff members tended to react defensively to criticism and did not respond adequately.

The senior personnel in the university, however, considered that the initial course validation and five-yearly course review procedures, together with the appointment of reputable external examiners, did work satisfactorily. The report also placed the partnership agreement in the context of the Burke proposals of 1974, which were considered to be "potentially extremely damaging to TCD". At that time it was expected that the proposed new NIHE Dublin would absorb the higher level programmes in the Colleges of Technology at Bolton Street and Kevin Street, and the College of Commerce at Rathmines. In 1975 the university was "already well advanced in working its policy towards an association" with that embryonic NIHE Dublin when the partnership agreement was finalised.

The report concluded that the relationship should continue but it recommended improvements in the operation of the partnership. Internal to TCD it recommended the appointment of an academic liaison officer, supported by a committee, to consider operational improvements. It also recommended the establishment of a joint academic council to enable staff members from TCD and the DIT colleges to contribute constructively to the partnership.

DIT/CDVEC review 1989–1990

In response to the TCD review report, the DIT/CDVEC initiated a review of the operation of the partnership agreement in 1989. The report that emerged in 1990 from this review surveyed the historical development of the partnership very much along the lines of the TCD review report, and, in particular, addressed the critical comments and recommendations in that report. It also considered the partnership in the new context of the government's 1985 Green Paper on Education[5] and the 1987 report of the International Study Group,[6] both outlined in Chapter 3. In this regard it explored the following possible future arrangements:

- discontinuation of the partnership agreement with TCD and the establishment of other arrangements
- the provision of greater autonomy for the DIT colleges with power to make their own awards to degree level
- the university and the DIT entering into a more formally structured relationship
- the continuation of the partnership, but with improvements in its operation.

CURRENT STAGE OF THE PARTNERSHIP

The prospect of the DIT being given the power to award degrees within a year or so was an integral element of the parliamentary discussions leading to enactment of the Dublin Institute of Technology Act 1992. During the academic year 1994/1995, the Liaison Council formed a working party to further review the partnership between the University of Dublin and the DIT and make suggestions on the future form of the relationship. The joint working party consisted of senior members of staff from both institutions.

A number of interim reports were forwarded to the Liaison Council who approved the final report in July 1998. It contained a number of recommendations.

In relation to courses that led to degrees of the university, it was agreed that from the student intake of September 1998, they would lead to degrees of the Institute. However, degrees of the university would be available to students who entered those courses in any year previous to that, regardless of their rate of passage through the course, within the regulations of the DIT. The related inter-colleges committees would continue to

---

5. *Partners in Education – Serving Community Needs* (Baile Átha Cliath: Oifig an tSoláthair), 1985.
6. *Technological Education, Report of the International Study Group to the Minister for Education* (Baile Átha Cliath: Oifig an tSoláthair), 1987.

meet as required until academic year 2000/2001 for four-year courses and until 2001/2002 for the five-year architecture course. Any of these courses undergoing five-yearly reviews up to summer 1999 would continue to have a joint DIT/TCD review panel, but thereafter would have a DIT panel on which a TCD staff member might serve as an external member. External examiners nominated for these courses would continue to be nominated jointly by the DIT and the university as indicated above.

All existing joint courses would continue as before, and new joint courses would be encouraged in the future.

The fee waiver scheme to enable DIT staff members to register for higher degrees of the university would continue and a reciprocal scheme for members of staff of the university to take courses in the Institute was agreed.

The seed funding scheme for joint research projects would be continued and focussed on first research initiatives of relatively recently appointed lecturers. In order to further assist the DIT in developing research, especially postgraduate research, it was agreed that at least one member of TCD staff, nominated by the Dean of Graduate Studies, would be appointed to membership of the Institute's Postgraduate Studies Committee.

It was also agreed that arrangements for staff from one institution to teach in the other would be encouraged, mainly at school and faculty level. Opportunities for sharing of facilities, for instance where purchases of large and expensive items of equipment might be involved, would also be welcomed and encouraged, generally on a case by case basis.

Finally it was agreed to review these arrangements during academic year 2000–2001.

SUMMARY

The partnership agreement between the Dublin colleges under the CDVEC and the University of Dublin, based on wide co-operation and commonality of interests, was signed in 1976. It ushered in a quarter century of growth in primary degree programmes and postgraduate research activities within the colleges.

The partnership represented a new and higher academic plateau for the DIT. This was especially so because the partnership was based on deep academic trust and commonality of interests at the time. This commonality arose to a large extent from the political and developmental problems facing the two parties and the partnership represented an imaginative response to the challenges of the time. It offered a welcome solution to the pressing need for additional degree places in Irish higher education in the 1970s, 1980s and 1990s. It effectively provided political support to the University of Dublin in its successful resistance to the Burke proposals. For the DIT it provided a viable alternative to its failure to benefit from the opportunities of the Ballymun Project. In depth and extent it was a unique collaborative venture between two academic institutions with different histories and ethos. It provided evidence of DIT's capacity to be the catalyst for change in the binary system of higher education.

Chapter 5

Dublin Institute of Technology Act 1992

The changing and developing nature of the activities of the colleges of the Dublin Institute of Technology (DIT) presented increasing problems for them in the 1980s as they sought to operate as effectively as possible as higher level institutions. These problems arose mainly from the restrictions imposed by the Vocational Education Act 1930 which was primarily intended to encompass a second level education provision. As the Institute began to engage in research and development work, difficulties arose that were highlighted in the study of the National Board for Science and Technology in 1981.[1] These restrictions may be seen in bold relief when the broad academic maturity that had been achieved by the Institute and its colleges at that stage is reviewed.

ACADEMIC MATURITY OF THE INSTITUTE AT THE START OF THE 1990s

The government Green Paper on Education, issued in 1985, stated that "the Institute has six constituent colleges and in terms of total enrolment is second in size only to UCD. . . Because of its size, its wide variety of courses in various disciplines, its national rather than regional character and the relationship which it already enjoys with the University of Dublin in regard to the award of degrees, the Institute is quite different in character from the Regional Technical Colleges (RTCs)".[2]

The International Study Group on Technological Education[3] in its report to the Minister for Education in 1987, stated that the Group "was impressed by the work of the (Dublin) colleges" and recognised "the high standing

---

1. *Barriers to Research and Development in the Higher Education Sector* (Dublin: National Board for Science and Technology), 1981.
2. *Partners in Education – Serving Community Needs, op. cit.*
3. *Technological Education, Report of the International Study Group to the Minister for Education, op. cit.*

which the colleges hold in their special fields of study — architecture, construction studies and mechanical engineering in Bolton Street; electronic engineering and science in Kevin Street; catering in Cathal Brugha Street; marketing and design in Mountjoy Square; business studies in Rathmines; music in Chatham Row".

It went on to state that:

> colleges of (the) DIT have been making their own academic awards for over 40 years. Industry and the professional bodies have recognised these awards and accepted them as bases for appointments to professional positions and admission to membership of professional bodies. ... The research activities of the DIT are wide ranging, as would be expected in an Institute of such diverse character. Collaboration with other researchers and institutions both nationally and internationally is a common feature of much research carried out by the Institute.

When the Dublin Institute of Technology Bill was being considered by Oireachtas Éireann in 1991 and 1992, statements praising the DIT and its academic standards were made by four successive Ministers for Education and other leading political spokespersons.

High level of demand for DIT full-time courses

For many years some 66 per cent of the 60,000 students who apply annually through the Central Applications Office (CAO) system for places on higher education courses had expressed a preference for a DIT course. This was by far the largest level of interest and support for courses offered by any higher education institution in the State. Chapter 8 gives an outline of the range of courses offered.

About two thirds of the full-time students admitted annually to the DIT entered diploma or certificate courses. The points scores of those who gained admission into these courses were very high by comparison with those obtaining places on courses in the Regional Technical Colleges (RTCs) and many of these applicants would have been eligible for admission to degree courses. The numbers of first preference applicants for its degree courses tended to be ahead of most of the universities. The points scores of those admitted to DIT degree courses were generally comparable with those of the universities. There was also a very high demand from DIT's own diploma and certificate graduates as well as from RTC graduates for the available places in the later stages of the degree courses, but usually only a small proportion of them could be accommodated due to the constraints of space and facilities.

Successful partnership with the University of Dublin

The DIT degree output under the partnership agreement, described in Chapter 4, rose from twenty-eight in 1975 to six hundred and six in 1992, a number larger than that of many of the universities. In 1992 there were twenty-eight full-time degree courses or course options and seven part-time degree courses offered in a wide range of key disciplines, and in total about 6,000 DIT students had qualified to receive University of Dublin degrees since the partnership was initiated in 1975.

Staff from each institution benefited mutually from working with each other by participating in course validations and reviews as well as various inter-colleges committees and other joint activities. By 1992, over fifty staff had achieved higher degrees in the University under the fee-waiver scheme developed under the partnership agreement. Arrangements existed for registering DIT postgraduate students with the University while they did their research work in the Institute under the supervision of DIT staff.

The standing of DIT graduates

DIT graduates were generally very successful in finding employment in the marketplace and often were favoured over university graduates because of their more applied expertise and knowledge. They were readily accepted for admission into the appropriate membership grades of a wide range of professional bodies in Ireland and internationally. Furthermore they were admitted to university postgraduate courses and programmes on the same basis as other university graduates. Some had gone on to achieve high academic distinction and appointment to university chairs in internationally prestigious academic institutions.

Notable features of DIT courses

While DIT degree courses shared many features in common with the universities such as minimum entry requirements, course duration and overall academic standards, they often had a different course structure with greater emphasis on practical knowledge, skills and project work and benefited from relatively small class groups. Within the DIT, courses were operated with a favourable student/staff ratio of about fourteen to one on average and usually close relationships developed between students and staff members that led to fruitful teaching and learning interactions between them. The Institute generally had extensive and modern specialised facilities to serve the needs of degree, diploma and certificate students as well as craft and apprentice students and by careful scheduling of classes in the different areas, the different student groups could be accommodated.

Development of research activities in the Institute

The Institute made significant progress in postgraduate research during the 1980s with the numbers of DIT postgraduate research students increasing significantly over that time. It had also taken a number of initiatives to encourage and support postgraduate research, expanding the industrial liaison function to provide greater support and developing policies for the development of research.

Quality assurance in the DIT

Formal academic quality assurance procedures had been developed and operated by the Academic Council across the Institute since 1970 and before, as described in Chapter 11. These procedures had been regularly reviewed and refined.

DIT staff expertise

Over the years priority had been given in recruitment in most areas to established professionals in their specialist disciplines. Many of the Institute's permanent academic staff had availed of the opportunities to enhance their qualifications since their recruitment and were involved in research or consultancy work appropriate to their discipline areas. Large numbers of staff members had participated in international exchanges through programmes such as Erasmus, Tempus and others. Staff commitment to the Institute, its courses and students was high, with low staff turnover and a good team spirit overall.

Academic maturity of the DIT and its schools

By general Irish standards in 1992, the DIT was a mature academic institution with a long history and tradition extending back over more than 100 years.

Most of its schools had been in existence for at least fifteen years and some for much longer than that. Influenced by the requirements of the Academic Council and involvement with the University of Dublin, professional bodies and other agencies including industry and business in the broadest sense, these schools were sensitive to the requirements of industry and the need to keep abreast of developments affecting their discipline areas.

Generally, DIT schools were rather large units responsible for operating a number of courses at different levels, with typical total enrolments of 250–500 full-time students and significantly higher numbers in some cases.

For more than forty years the different DIT colleges and their schools employed leading academics and professional practitioners as external examiners and consultants as a vital element of peer review. These experts, drawn from Ireland and abroad, made significant contributions over the years to the development of courses as well as helping to assure their quality and standards.

The Institute had long attached priority to having its courses accredited or recognised by the professional bodies appropriate to its discipline areas. In virtually all cases DIT courses met in full the academic requirements for membership, or at least merited the same level of exemptions as comparable university courses.

Need for greater autonomy

The difficulties in relation to developing research, development and consultancy activities in the Institute, growing since the 1970s, were emphasised in the report on technological education by the International Study Group in 1987. This report recommended that statutory provision should be made for the Institute to engage in this type of work and that it should be encouraged to make its expertise and facilities more widely available to industry and business as considered appropriate. This report also recommended that the DIT should be established on a statutory basis and that its financing should be provided as a block grant through the Higher Education Authority (HEA), as in the case of the universities.

OBJECTIVES OF THE DUBLIN INSTITUTE OF TECHNOLOGY BILL 1991

The Dublin Institute of Technology Bill, brought forward by the Department of Education in 1991 in close consultation with senior members of staff of the Institute and its parent City of Dublin Vocational Education Committee (CDVEC), sought to address these and other needs of DIT, while having regard to the following:

• the provision to the Institute of appropriate freedom and autonomy to function as a third level institution, while maintaining some links with the CDVEC system and remaining on the technological side of the binary system

- the provision of a satisfactory legal basis and capacity to engage in research and enter into arrangements, including participation in limited companies, so as to exploit fully the results of such activity

- while the six DIT colleges had been functioning under the CDVEC as complementary rather than competing institutions, each having its own management structure and range of disciplines, they had a formally established Academic Council as far back as 1970. In 1978 the DIT was established with its own Governing Body as a sub-committee of the CDVEC and it functioned well as a loose federal arrangement. A further major step was needed however, if the DIT was to become a single, autonomous, integrated higher education institution

- the CDVEC colleges had been making their own certificate and diploma awards since the 1950s and while these were widely recognised nationally and internationally by employers, professional bodies and academic institutions, they did not have an appropriate statutory basis. In relation to degree awards the fruitful partnership agreement, entered into with the University of Dublin (TCD) in 1976, had benefited several thousand DIT graduates, but there were concerns as to whether this arrangement was appropriate for such a large and diverse institution as the DIT in the medium and longer term.

POLITICAL ATTITUDES TO THE DUBLIN INSTITUTE OF TECHNOLOGY BILL

The basic content and format of the Dublin Institute of Technology Bill 1991 was almost identical to the University of Limerick and Dublin City University Acts 1989. During the protracted period while the Bill was being processed, from November 1991 when the second stage was introduced in Dáil Éireann until July 1992 when it was finally approved by Seanad Éireann, there were three different Ministers for Education — Mary O'Rourke, Noel Davern and Séamus Brennan. The Minister of State in the Department of Education, Liam Aylward, was also involved. The main education spokespersons for the different opposition parties participated actively in the debate.

The statements of these spokespersons on the Institute and the Bill as it moved through the Oireachtas, reflected the deep appreciation within Irish society of the considerable service and achievement of the DIT and indicated the high standing of the DIT colleges in the wider community.

Only one aspect of the Bill divided the government spokespersons and those of all the opposition parties — the timing of the granting of degree awarding power to the Institute. The opposition side favoured the inclusion of this power in the Act while the government position, enshrined in Section 5.2(a) of the Act, was that this function "which may include the function of conferring degrees, postgraduate degrees and honorary awards ... may be assigned to it, from time to time, by order made ..." by the Minister for Education, but possibly within twelve months. There appeared to be unanimous agreement that this power was fully merited, as is evident from the official Dáil and Seanad debates.

Minister for Education, Mary O'Rourke TD

Introducing the second stage of the DIT Bill on 7 November 1991, the then Minister for Education, Mary O'Rourke TD, said:

> Section 3 of the DIT Bill provides for the establishment of the Institute and that it will be constituted from the six existing colleges. . . The principal function will be to provide vocational and technical education and training for the economic, technological, scientific, commercial, industrial, social and cultural development of the State. . . . Provision is also made for engaging in research, consultancy and development work. . . The DIT will, subject to the recommendation of the Academic Council, retain the power to award its own diplomas, certificates and other awards. . . Degree awarding powers could at the appropriate time be assigned to the DIT. . .

Response of Teresa Ahearne TD

Responding on the same occasion, Teresa Ahearne TD, the higher education spokesperson for Fine Gael, the largest opposition party, said:

> The colleges, in particular the DIT, at this stage rightly claim to have long experience of teaching to degree level... I suggest that now is the time to give the colleges this power to award their own degrees.

Other participants in the Oireachtas debate

In November 1991, the new Minister for Education, Noel Davern TD, defended the government's position on delaying the granting of degree awarding power, while acknowledging the Institute's high reputation.

On the opposition side a wide range of deputies, including the education spokespersons of all the opposition parties — Fine Gael, Labour and Democratic Left — supported an amendment to the Bill, to include degree awarding power.

The debate concluded in July 1992 and the then Minister for Education, Séamus Brennan TD, maintained the government's position but suggested "the delay in awarding degrees for a targeted period of twelve months".

The DIT Bill was processed through Seanad Éireann, also in July 1992, before it received final approval on 10 July. Much of the discussion in the Seanad also concerned the issue of degree awarding power for the Institute.

Responding to the debate, Minister for Education Séamus Brennan TD, said on 10 July 1992:

> The DIT will be given degree awarding powers and my target, subject to discussions, would be that within twelve months, we might be able to arrive at that position. . . (We) are undertaking a major reorganisation of the DIT, the integration of the six colleges into a single structure. . . It is appropriate that, before we take that final step we should have an opportunity to consult with the new Governing Body and the Academic Council as to qualitative matters and, generally, how we might proceed. . .

Despite the Minister's commitment, almost five years were to elapse before these powers were granted in April 1997. Before these powers were assigned, the Institute was required to undertake an audit of its quality assurance procedures (see Chapter 11). It is possible that the Department of Education delayed the process of assigning degree awarding powers to the DIT because this might have been seen as a step towards university status for the Institute and a dismantling of the binary system in higher education. This might certainly be deduced from the role set out for the DIT in the Qualifications (Education and Training) Act 1999, which was then in preparation.

AMENDMENTS MADE TO THE DIT LEGISLATION BY THE OIREACHTAS

A large number of amendments were introduced as the DIT Bill was processed through the Oireachtas during 1991 and 1992.

Greater autonomy for the Institute

Some amendments were introduced in response to the concerns raised during the Dáil debate, about the inclusion in relation to many functions of the Institute of the phrase "subject to such conditions as the Minister may determine". It was felt that this would undermine the main thrust of the new legislation, which was to give the Institute greater autonomy in managing its own affairs. The DIT Bill was amended to exclude this phrase in many areas. Another important change gave the title of president to the chief officer of the Institute, rather than director, which is used in the RTCs. Provision was also made for the appointment of a number of directors in DIT, with each of them answerable to the president.

Preparing the Institute for conferring its own degree awards

Section 5.1(b) of the Bill was amended and in the Act reads as follows: "to confer, grant or give diplomas, certificates or other educational awards, excluding degrees other than degrees provided for by order under subsection (2)(a)".

Section 5.2(a) of the DIT Bill was also amended to read as follows in the Act: "The Institute shall have such other functions, which may include the function of conferring degrees, postgraduate degrees and honorary awards as may be assigned to it, from time to time, by order made. . ."

The Institute, under the legislation enacted, was also allowed to continue "to enter into arrangements with the National Council for Educational Awards, with any university in the State or with any other authority approved by the Minister from time to time, for the purpose of having degrees, diplomas, certificates or other educational awards conferred, granted or given".

The DIT Bill 1991 was enacted by the Oireachtas in July 1992 as the Dublin Institute of Technology Act 1992.

OUTLINE OF THE PROVISIONS OF THE DUBLIN INSTITUTE OF TECHNOLOGY ACT 1992

Having been approved by both Houses of the Oireachtas, the Dublin Institute of Technology Act became law when it was signed by Her Excellency, the President, Mary Robinson, before the end of July 1992.

Unification of the six colleges

The Act provided for the establishment of the Institute, constituted from the six colleges at Adelaide Road/Chatham Row, Bolton Street, Cathal Brugha Street, Kevin Street, Mountjoy Square and Rathmines. Provision was also made for the possible incorporation of other educational institutions into the Institute in the future.

Functions of the new Institute

The Act set out the functions of the Institute, the principal one being to provide vocational and technical education and training for the economic, technological, scientific, commercial, industrial, social and cultural development of the State. To this end the Institute was to provide courses of study and might enter into arrangements with appropriate authorities for the award of degrees, diplomas, certificates and other educational awards.

Provision was also made for the Institute to engage in research, consultancy and development work, either on its own or with other institutions and to provide services in relation to such work and enter into arrangements, including participation in limited companies, to exploit the results of this work. The Institute, subject to the recommendations of its Academic Council, retained the power to award its own diplomas and certificates but the capacity to make degree awards was not granted to it. Additional functions could be assigned to it however by order of the Minister made with the concurrence of the Minister for Finance and the approval of both Houses of the Oireachtas. These included degree awarding powers, in accordance with the provisions of the Act.

Composition and functions of the Governing Body

The Act provided for the establishment of a Governing Body with a composition comprising a chairperson, eighteen ordinary members and the president of the Institute. Of these, six persons were to be nominated by the CDVEC, two were to be members of the academic staff, one a representative of the non-academic staff, two students of the Institute, one person nominated by the Irish Congress of Trade Unions, one nominated by TCD and five by such other organisations and interests as the CDVEC considered requiring representation, having regard to the particular courses in the Institute and the overall membership of the Governing Body. These provisions were modified somewhat in the DIT (Amendment) Act 1994 to facilitate gender equity and to provide Academic Council with a role in the nomination process for the five organisations or interests requiring representation.

It is somewhat unfortunate that the composition of the Governing Body did not provide a more even balance between academic and other representation, as would be appropriate for an institution on the verge of obtaining degree awarding powers. The composition assigned would appear to indicate a desire by the Department of Education to limit the autonomy of the Institute and ensure a continuing high level of control by the Department.

The Act set out the functions of the Governing Body which were to be exercised in accordance with the general policy and the programmes and budget approved annually. The functions included managing the affairs of the Institute, including its land and buildings and performing such functions as were conferred on the Institute by the Act. It also provided that the Governing Body might appoint committees and would have regard to national aims in relation to the Irish language and culture.

Procedures for appointing staff

The Act specified the procedures for the appointment of the president and directors of the Institute as well as other staff. The Third Schedule to the Act related specifically to the president's role and functions. It also set out more general provisions in relation to the selection and appointment of staff and their conditions of employment and superannuation arrangements. There were also special provisions that would apply to existing staff who transferred from the CDVEC to the Institute on its establishment.

Appointment and functions of the Academic Council

The Act provided for the appointment by the Governing Body of a statutory Academic Council and prescribed the functions of this Council. These included provision for designing, developing and assisting the implementation of courses of study, making recommendations on programmes for research and development work and acting in relation to the selection, admission, retention and exclusion of students.

Annual programmes, budgets and reports

The Act included provisions in relation to the annual submission, approval and implementation of programmes and budgets for the Institute and the preparation and submission of an annual report. It also made provision for such other information as might be required. It provided that annual grants might be paid to the Institute out of moneys provided by the Oireachtas and specified that it must keep proper accounts which would have to be submitted annually to the Comptroller and Auditor General. The Institute might charge fees or make other appropriate charges for its services.

Transfer of property and liabilities from CDVEC

The Act also dealt with the transfer to the Institute of property and liabilities held or incurred by the CDVEC before the establishment date. Contracts in force and legal proceedings pending before the establishment date were preserved or continued by substituting the name of the Institute for that of the CDVEC.

COMPARISON OF THE DIT ACT WITH THE REGIONAL TECHNICAL COLLEGES ACT 1992

The DIT and RTC Acts, passed at approximately the same time in 1992, had much in common, with the same general structure and identical wording in several sections.

Awarding powers

One of the special features of the DIT legislation was that it gave to the Institute the power to confer its own academic awards, unlike the RTC legislation which did not have such a provision. Sections 5.1(b) and 5.2(a) of the DIT Act gave to the Institute the function of granting certificates, diplomas and, possibly through a ministerial order, the power to grant primary, postgraduate and honorary degrees. In fact, as described in Chapter 11, the power to confer degrees was given to the DIT in 1997. Section 5.3 read thus:

> Awards under the provisions of subsection 1(b) or under any function in relation to degrees which may be assigned to the Institute by order made under subsection 2 may only be conferred, granted or given on the recommendation of the Academic Council to or on persons who satisfy the Academic Council that they have attended or otherwise pursued or followed appropriate courses of study, instruction, research or training provided by the Institute, or by such other institution as the Minister on the recommendation of the Governing Body may approve, and have attained an appropriate standard in examinations or other tests of knowledge or ability or have performed

other exercises in a manner regarded by the Academic Council as satisfactory.

In the case of the RTCs, their legislation required them "to enter into arrangements with the National Council for Educational Awards, with any university in the State or with any other authority approved by the Minister from time to time for the purpose of having degrees, diplomas, certificates or other educational awards conferred, granted or given and to make such other arrangements as may be approved by the Minister from time to time for this purpose".

Different Academic Council functions

In the DIT legislation, provisions relating to the Academic Council, in addition to those in the RTC Act, included the following:

* according to Section 11.3(c), the Academic Council was empowered "to make recommendations in accordance with section 5(3) of this Act"
* according to Section 11.3(h), the Academic Council was required "to make recommendations to the Governing Body in relation to the appointment of external examiners"
* according to Section 11.3(i), the Academic Council had the function "to make recommendations to the Governing Body in relation to the conferment of honorary awards".

These provisions gave important functions to the DIT's Academic Council which were consistent with the DIT making its own awards.

COMPARISON OF THE DIT ACT WITH THE ACTS ESTABLISHING DUBLIN CITY UNIVERSITY AND UNIVERSITY OF LIMERICK

The 1989 legislation which established the University of Limerick (UL) was almost identical in format and wording, and was enacted simultaneously, with that of Dublin City University (DCU).

Awarding powers

Under their earlier 1980 legislation neither of these institutions, as NIHEs, had any academic awarding powers. While one of their main functions was "to provide degree level courses, diploma level courses and certificate level courses and, subject to such conditions as the Minister may prescribe, such other courses, including postgraduate courses, as may seem appropriate to the Governing Body ...", that legislation prescribed that these were courses leading to awards of the NCEA. Hence, until their university legislation was enacted in 1989, both NIHEs were precluded from making their own academic awards. This was in contrast to the DIT situation, in that its colleges began making their own certificate and diploma awards some thirty years earlier, in the late 1950s.

Similarity of the DIT Act 1992 and the DCU Act 1989

When the legislative framework of the DIT is compared with that of the newer universities, the two sets of provisions are almost identical, with the exception of the DIT's capacity to award its own degrees being deferred pending its formal establishment and the Minister being satisfied that suitable arrangements are in place in relation to its new structures and operations.

In the UL and DCU Acts, the new universities were given the functions:

(ii) to confer, grant or give degrees, diplomas, certificates or other educational awards, on the recommendation of the Academic Council, to or on persons who satisfy the Academic Council that they have attended or otherwise pursued or followed appropriate courses of study, instruction or research provided by the University, or by such other colleges or institutions as the Governing Body may approve, and have attained an appropriate standard in examinations or other tests of knowledge or ability or have performed other exercises in a manner regarded by the Academic Council as satisfactory,

(iii) to confer honorary degrees on persons in such manner and subject to such conditions as the Governing Body, after consultation with the Academic Council, may deem appropriate, and

(iv) to enter into arrangements with other relevant institutions inside and outside the State for the purposes of offering joint courses and of conducting research and development work and to enter into arrangements, including participation in limited liability companies, for the purpose of exploiting the results of research and development work undertaken by the University either separately or jointly.

With the ministerial order of 1997 giving degree awarding power to the DIT up to the highest postgraduate level, the Institute's legislative base is almost identical with that of the 1989 legislation of the new universities.

Appointing external examiners

Under their university legislation in 1989 the new universities were in a position to make recommendations to their Governing Bodies in relation to the appointment of external examiners. Until then this was a function of the NCEA as the body responsible for making academic awards to students successfully completing their courses.

Summary

The Dublin Institute Technology Act 1992, and as amended in 1994, set the statutory foundations for the independent unified Institute, with power to confer certificate, diploma and, as later amended by ministerial order in 1996, degree awards. In the words of the Minister for State in the Department of Education, Liam Aylward TD, in introducing the Bill to Seanad Éireann, the Act acknowledged "the outstanding contribution which the Institute (had) made in the field of higher education" and laid "the foundation for the future development of the Institute in a new and unified structure which (would) build on the solid base of achievement of individual colleges".

This Act had some advantages over the parallel RTC Act, compared favourably with the previous NIHE Acts and was virtually identical with the DCU and UL Acts 1989. The discussions in the Oireachtas on the DIT Bill indicated the wide political recognition of the high academic reputation of DIT and its role in higher education.

The Oireachtas debate, and its culmination in the DIT Act 1992 itself, were the most significant high-water mark in the academic development and recognition of the Institute up to that time. Nevertheless the DIT Act set limits to the autonomy of the Institute and largely continued the earlier fairly direct and strong control of its activities by the Department of Education.

Chapter 6

Organisational Development of the Institute under the DIT Act 1992

The Dublin Institute of Technology Act 1992 established a statutory basis for the Institute to function as an autonomous higher education institution. The DIT Act was to have wide-ranging effects on the structure, operation and identity of the Institute, and these continue to unfold. This chapter examines and documents these unfolding effects.

ESTABLISHMENT OF THE INSTITUTE ON A STATUTORY BASIS

The Dublin Institute of Technology (DIT) was duly established on a formal basis with effect from 1 January 1993, constituted from the six third-level colleges in central Dublin which had been operating under the aegis of the City of Dublin Vocational Education Committee (CDVEC). Mr Michael O'Donnell, who had filled the post of director of the Institute for over a decade since 1982 in an *ad hoc*, part-time capacity in addition to being principal of the College of Technology Bolton Street, was appointed as acting president of the Institute. The principals of the other five colleges were appointed first directors of the Institute in accordance with the provisions of the DIT Act.[1] The Institute entered into arrangements with its former parent body, the CDVEC, to have it continue to provide administrative services relating to personnel, payroll and payment of creditors on an interim basis.

The key co-ordinating committee within the Institute, the Executive Council, had been functioning since the Institute was informally established in 1978. It had consisted of the principals of the six constituent colleges, with the chairperson selected from among them acting also as the informal director. With the implementation of the DIT Act in 1993 the

---

1. *Annual Report, 1 January 1993-31 August 1994* (Dublin: Dublin Institute of Technology), 1994.

Executive Council became the Directorate, comprising the president and directors and chaired by the president, it took on an enhanced role.

INSTITUTE OF PUBLIC ADMINISTRATION CONSULTATION ON STRUCTURES 1992–1993

In late 1992, before the Institute was formally established, the Department of Education engaged the Institute for Public Administration (IPA) as consultants to review the operations of the Institute. The IPA was asked to "make recommendations as to its reorganisation and rationalisation on the basis of consistent faculties or schools, and the appropriate campus placement of such faculties or schools." The Department of Education also asked the IPA to recommend "the appropriate senior management structure for the Institute below the level of president". It was asked to recommend other structures, including "reporting arrangements and related staffing of central services for the Institute answerable to senior management, to include financial and accounting services, admissions, personnel management, information technology (including central library services), facilities management, external services (including industrial liaison), student counselling, careers and appointments, medical and other student welfare services". Finally the IPA was also asked to recommend the numbers of administrative staff and their grades which should transfer from the CDVEC, recognising that some of them were already engaged in providing services to the colleges and their staffs in relation to accounting, personnel and other areas which would in future be the responsibility of the Institute itself.

The IPA consultants engaged in wide discussions with the staff of the colleges, particularly those at senior levels, as well as with the Chief Executive Officer of the CDVEC and some of its other senior officers. They also held discussions with senior representatives of three Irish universities, University College Cork, Dublin City University and the University of Limerick and two UK universities, Manchester Metropolitan University and the University of North London.

The IPA consultants produced two reports. The first of these related specifically to the transition from the aegis of the CDVEC to the new independent situation and in particular the transfer of administrative staff from CDVEC to the Institute. It recommended that sixteen such staff, mainly in junior administrative grades, should be transferred to the DIT.

The second report, published in April 1993, was more extensive and addressed the main terms of reference given to the consultants. It presented a detailed set of recommendations relating to proposed administrative structures for the new autonomous Institute.

Administrative structures recommended for the Institute

The core recommendation in the second report was that the DIT should be reorganised on the basis of six broad discipline-based faculties, each of which would be headed by a director. There would be four other senior Institute posts at director level which would encompass an Institute secretary, a finance director, a director of academic affairs and a director of external affairs. This would entail a fundamental change from the previous interdisciplinary college structure to a new faculty structure, but it had been heralded in the Governing Body review of the DIT in 1983 and widely discussed across the Institute in the intervening years.[2] The consultants analysed many of the issues facing the Institute in making this change and achieving a cohesive and integrated structure. They endeavoured to formulate recommendations which were likely to find wide acceptance, by retaining the better features and practices of the previous situation. At the same time they sought to provide the Institute with an appropriate administrative structure to serve the needs of a large, comprehensive and modern university level institution. In the report they drew attention to some of the difficulties that might be encountered in implementing the new structure and some of the problems of change that would face the existing staff.

Initial response of Governing Body to the report

The Governing Body broadly accepted the report but recognised that one of its first tasks was to provide the Institute with an appropriate management and operational structure that would have the broad support of staff. It was realised that the key person in the detailed formulation and implementation of the new structure would be the president and chief officer of the Institute. Therefore the Governing Body postponed detailed decisions on the IPA report and its recommendations until this appointment was made.

---

2. *Report on Governing Body Seminar* (Dublin: City of Dublin Vocational Education Committee), February 1983.

DEVELOPING THE CENTRAL OFFICES

Over the first six months the DIT held interviews for the appointment of the president, the post having been advertised in October 1992. The Institute's first budget and operational programme were prepared and submitted in accordance with the provisions of the DIT Act. Discussions in relation to staff structures and the transfer of some administrative staff from the CDVEC head office, following negotiations in that regard between CDVEC and the Department of Education, also took place. Arrangements were made during this period to rent Fitzwilliam House, 30 Upper Pembroke Street, as a central office building for the new Institute. It was projected that there would be a central office staff of about sixty people, including the office of the president and other key administrative and service offices.

The Governing Body, at its June 1993 meeting, appointed Dr Brendan Goldsmith, who had been vice-principal of the College of Technology, Kevin Street, as president of the Institute. He took up duty in the post from 1 September 1993 on a ten-year contract.

GOVERNING BODY'S CONSULTATIVE GROUP TO REVIEW THE APPLICATION OF THE IPA REPORT PROPOSALS

In accordance with the DIT Act, the Governing Body, in association with the president, had responsibility for determining and implementing the most appropriate administrative structure for the Institute, subject to guidelines and regulations issued by the Minister for Education. After extensive discussions on the IPA report, the Governing Body established a consultative group, which included the president and was chaired by a member of the Governing Body.

This consultative group was required to carry out an extensive consultation process with staff at various levels in relation to the proposals in the IPA report. The aim was to draw out the implications of the proposals, remove ambiguities and enhance the understanding and general acceptability of the changes proposed. On behalf of the consultative group, the Institute secretary and another senior officer attended meetings with the staff of each school and department and also met with other interest groups, including trade union representatives. In addition the IPA consultants were engaged by the Institute to interact with a wide cross-section of Institute staff through a series of workshops to obtain feedback on their reactions to and concerns about the recommendations of the report. This consultation process extended over a period of several months. During that time seventy written submissions were received from staff members.

Approval of the report of the consultative group

The consultative group finally presented its report on the consultation process to the Governing Body in late 1994. This report, in broad terms, endorsed the recommendations in the original IPA report, while modifying or clarifying some of the recommendations and dealing more closely with the actual situation in some schools. At a special meeting in October 1994, the Governing Body accepted and endorsed the consultative group's report, with some further modifications.

A copy of the report as approved was forwarded to the Minister for Education for information.[3] It was recognised that its implementation had significant additional funding implications, estimated to be in excess of £1 million per annum.

The report was prepared in the absence of an institutional mission statement or, more significantly, a strategic plan. There was no provision in the report for rotation of senior posts in the Institute, and while this may have been dictated by the provisions of the DIT Act and by contractual obligations to structured members of staff, the issue had historically been a source of contention among lecturing staff. Some sections of staff were uneasy with aspects of the structures proposed in the report because they felt that their views, expressed in the consultation process, were not taken into account. The titles chosen for some of the faculties and their constituent schools caused concern, particularly among staff members directly affected by changes proposed.

FACULTY STRUCTURE FOR THE INSTITUTE

Basic structure proposed

In accordance with this report, approved by the Governing Body, the Institute would be reorganised into six broad subject or discipline based faculties. The proposed titles of the faculties underwent some modification to become as follows, with the schools to be allocated to each faculty given after the titles of the faculties:

---

3. *Faculty Structures in Dublin Institute of Technology* (Dublin: Dublin Institute of Technology), 1994.

- applied arts — art and design, media and communications, modern languages, music and drama, social and legal studies
- built environment — architecture, construction studies, environmental technology, property studies
- business — accountancy, distribution, management, marketing
- engineering — civil and building services, control and electrical, electronic and communications, mechanical
- science — biological sciences, chemistry, mathematics and informatics, physics
- tourism and food — food operations, food science and technology, tourism services.

Each school might have a number of component departments. The apprenticeship or trade area associated with each faculty or discipline (if any) would be integrated with or placed under the aegis of the appropriate school.

The faculty director appointed for each faculty would represent the views of that faculty at the Directorate. She/he would also be responsible for managing and co-ordinating the implementation of the policies of the Institute on budgetary, academic quality assurance and other matters at faculty level, as well as managing the business of the faculty. The senior management of each faculty would consist of the faculty director, the heads of school in the faculty, the heads of departments within the schools, other structured post-holders and the faculty administrator. Within each faculty there would be two organisational arms, a faculty executive and a faculty board.

The faculty executive, consisting of the director, the heads of school and the faculty administrator, would be the management team for the faculty and have particular responsibility for the budget and resources of the faculty.

The faculty board, consisting of the director, the heads of school, the chairpersons of all its course committees, at least two students and up to two co-opted members, would have general responsibility for the implementation of academic quality assurance procedures and other academic policies within the faculty.

Each faculty would be supported by an administrative structure headed by a faculty administrator who would have responsibilities relating to faculty accounts, registration, records and examinations. Each school would have its own secretarial support.

The Directorate of the Institute would comprise the president, the six faculty directors and the other four central directors with institutional functions (secretary, academic affairs, finance and external affairs).

The president's functions, set out in the third schedule of the DIT Act, were "subject to the provisions of the Act, (to) control and direct the staff of the Institute in the implementation of such activities and be responsible to the Governing Body therefor and for the efficient and proper management of the Institute . . . be a member of the Governing Body . . . be a member of the Academic Council. . ."

It would be the responsibility of the director of finance to supply and develop advanced financial management systems. Financial planning, budgetary policy, systems development and financial control would all fall within the remit.

The secretary would be responsible for the Governing Body secretariat, the operation of the Institute's personnel policies, its buildings and maintenance services and for support to the teaching services of the Institute.

The director of academic affairs would have institutional responsibility for academic affairs, working with senior academic staff in promoting the academic quality, relevance and development of the full range of the Institute's courses and programmes. This director would be responsible for assembling and evaluating information relating to curricular developments, for putting appropriate academic and administrative systems in place and for monitoring their operation.

The director of external affairs would have responsibility for the development of the Institute's links with industry and the community, for the promotion and exploitation of applied research and consultancy and for other associated services, including fund-raising. The remit would embrace the more commercially and industrially oriented activities of the Institute and its enterprises.

APPOINTMENT OF THE DIRECTORS

In September 1993, the Governing Body decided that one of the first directors, Robert Lawlor, who had been principal of the College of Catering in Cathal Brugha Street, would take up the post of Institute Secretary. He and his colleagues Frank Brennan, James Hickey and Frank Heneghan, who had been principals of the College of Technology, Kevin Street, the College of Commerce, Rathmines, and the College of Music, Adelaide Road/Chatham Row respectively, became first directors of the Institute with the implementation of the DIT Act. At that time the post of director of finance of the Institute was advertised and in due course filled by Margaret Davin in 1994. Some *ad hoc* arrangements were made, with the approval of the Governing Body and the Department of Education, to fill vacant director posts through acting appointments.

In 1995 approval was received from the Department of Education to fill the other posts at director level, including the faculty directors and the directors of academic affairs and external affairs. These posts were filled during 1996. Frank Brennan was appointed as director of the faculty of engineering and after the other permanent director appointments had been made, the following were the directors at the start of academic year 1996/1997:

Applied arts	Dr Ellen Hazelkorn
Built environment	Mr John Ratcliffe
Business	Mr Paul O'Sullivan
Engineering	Mr Frank Brennan
Science	Dr Matthew Hussey
Tourism and food	Mr Michael Mulvey
Secretary	Mr Robert Lawlor
Finance	Mr Ray Wills
External affairs	Dr Declan Glynn
Academic affairs	Dr David Gillingham.

ACADEMIC COUNCIL

In accordance with the DIT Act, the Institute has a statutory Academic Council appointed by the Governing Body. The Academic Council assists the Governing Body in the planning, co-ordinating, developing and overseeing of the educational work of the Institute and in protecting, maintaining and developing the academic standards of the courses and other activities of the Institute.

Membership

The Governing Body decided that the DIT Academic Council would have the following membership (fifty-four in total) and composition: four *ex officio* members (president, directors of academic affairs and external affairs, chief librarian), thirty-four faculty representatives, thirteen elected staff representatives and three student representatives.

The Academic Council would be required to meet three or four times per annum. Its meetings would be chaired by the president, the director of academic affairs, or the president's nominee.

However, pending the implementation of the complete faculty structures, it was agreed to retain the existing pre-1992 Academic Council structure. At the time of writing in March 2000, this remains the situation.

INTERIM ADMINISTRATION OF THE INSTITUTE

The colleges had developed different internal committee structures, as previously outlined, and some of these were continued in the new DIT. However following the adoption of the first edition of the quality assurance handbook by the Academic Council in March 1995 and pending the implementation of the complete faculty structures, each college site established a college Academic Board to perform the academic and quality assurance functions envisaged for a Faculty Board, in relation to the courses in the college.[4] Each college also had a college Executive Board consisting of the director, senior academic staff (mostly at senior lecturer II level) and a secretary/registrar (retitled as faculty administrator in 1997) to advise the director and assist in the general management of the college.

DEVELOPMENT OF A MISSION STATEMENT FOR THE INSTITUTE

The general functions of the Institute are specified in the DIT Act. However, the Governing Body discussed and reviewed its general mission, aims and goals and in 1994 adopted the following as the Institute's brief statement of mission, derived from the Act:

> The Dublin Institute of Technology is a comprehensive higher educational institution, fulfilling a national and international role in providing full-time and part-time educational programmes across the whole spectrum of higher education. It aims to achieve this in an innovative, responsive, caring and flexible learning environment. It is committed to providing access to students of all ages and backgrounds, and to achieving quality and excellence in all aspects of its work. This commitment extends to the provision of research, product development and consultancy services for industry and society,

---

4. *Quality Assurance Handbook* (Dublin: Dublin Institute of Technology), 1995.

> while continuing to have regard to the technological, commercial, social and cultural needs of the community it serves.

QUALITY ASSURANCE AUDIT LEADING TO THE AUTHORITY TO CONFER DEGREES

The Dublin Institute of Technology Act 1992 made provision for a ministerial order from the Minister for Education for the DIT to be given the power to make degree awards. Indeed, in 1992 when the legislation was being moved through the Oireachtas, the Minister for Education anticipated that this power might well be given to the Institute within twelve months, when progress in integrating the six colleges into the Institute and in developing academic quality assurance procedures had been achieved. In 1995, in order to assist the then Minister, Niamh Bhreathnach TD, to reach a determination on granting this power to the Institute, she requested the Higher Education Authority (HEA) to carry out an institutional and systems review or audit of the quality assurance procedures in place in the Institute and the effectiveness of their operation.

This quality audit, preceded by a thorough institutional self-evaluation, was carried out during academic year 1995/1996 and is described in some detail in Chapter 11. The outcome of the process was the ministerial order of May 1997 granting degree awarding power to the highest postgraduate level to the DIT. This was the highest level of academic recognition and accreditation achieved by the autonomous DIT and was a major boost to the morale of staff throughout the Institute.

REVIEW OF THE DIT FOR DESIGNATION AS A UNIVERSITY UNDER SECTION 9 OF THE UNIVERSITIES ACT 1997–1998

An important aspect of the definition of a university is the power to award degrees at primary and postgraduate levels. A dictionary definition of a university is "an institution of higher education that provides facilities for full-time teaching and research and is authorised to grant academic degrees".[5] However, the Universities Act 1997 declared that an educational institution in Ireland, other than one designated under the Act, in future might not use the title "university" without the approval of the Minister for Education. Section 9 of the same Act provided that a new university

---

5.   *Chambers 21st Century Dictionary* (Edinburgh: Chambers), 1996.

could be established by order of the Government, after the advice of a body of experts and the HEA has been considered.

The Governing Body of the DIT, with the agreement of the Academic Council, determined in 1996 to seek designation as a university under the Universities Bill, then being processed through the Oireachtas. This course of action followed logically from the developments in the Institute over the previous thirty years. The developments under the partnership with the University of Dublin, the terms of the DIT Act, the consolidation of six colleges into a unified Institute and the institutional quality assurance audit leading to degree-awarding powers were all clear indicators of achievement and success along the way. Furthermore, the review team's report recommended that "the relevant authorities should consider whether key features of the (university) legislation should be extended to the DIT and its legislation . . . amended in the light" of this. In particular, the review team noted that "the current conditions attached to funding and operation of the Institute impose significant constraints on the freedom of the Institute to manage its day to day operations. In terms of promoting quality improvement, for example, these constraints are particularly obvious in relation to the deployment and development of staff."[6] The terms of the Universities Act would provide the autonomy required by the Institute to overcome these constraints.

The definition of a university does not preclude there being a range of programmes leading to non-degree awards in a university. Such programmes are widespread in universities in Ireland and internationally. In seeking designation as a university, the Governing Body was committed to maintaining the multi-level character of the Institute – catering for apprenticeship programmes, certificate and diploma courses, as well as undergraduate and postgraduate degree programmes and providing opportunities for students to transfer by clear academic ladders between these different levels.

Appointment and work of the review group

The Minister for Education, Niamh Bhreathnach TD, agreed in May 1997 to the appointment of a review group by the HEA, to investigate and advise on whether the DIT should be designated as a university.

The review group was appointed by Mícheál Martin TD, the new Minister for Education and Science, in July 1997, in accordance with Section

6. *Review of Quality Assurance Procedures in the Dublin Institute of Technology: Report of the International Review Team* (Dublin: Higher Education Authority), 1996.

9 of the Universities Act. The membership of the group is given below. While the review group was being formed, acting on the invitation of the HEA, the Institute submitted a document providing an introductory outline of the Institute and its recent development.

Members of the Review Group 1997–1998

Chairperson
Dermot Nally, former Secretary to the Government

Members
Prof. Máire Mulcahy, University College Cork
Prof. Eda Sagarra, University of Dublin
Prof. Malcolm Skilbeck, formerly Deputy Director, OECD (previously Vice-Chancellor, Deakin University, Australia)
Dr J. K. M. Gevers, President, University of Amsterdam
Mary Finan, Managing Director, Wilson Hartnell Public Relations Ltd (immediate past President, Dublin Chamber of Commerce)
Brian Sweeney, Chairperson, Siemens (Ireland) Ltd

Secretary
Mary Kerr, HEA

Terms of reference

The terms of reference given to the group required it, in consultation with the Institute:

- to establish a schedule for the review process, to include the timing for submission of material by the Institute and the timing and anticipated duration of visits to the Institute

- to establish such criteria as it considered appropriate as the basis for its review and assessment, to be notified to the Institute for any comments the Institute might wish to offer

- to establish such material and information as the group might require the Institute to furnish to facilitate its review and assessment

- while otherwise determining its own working procedures, to ensure that its advice should be of the form of a report which should, *inter alia,* detail the extent to which the Institute, as constituted and functioning, discharged the various objects and functions of a university in accordance with sections 12 and 13 of the Universities Act.

Deliberations of the group

In preparation for the first meeting of the review group in September 1997, the chairperson invited the Institute to submit a second document outlining the ways in which the Institute already functioned as a university and the main reasons why it sought to be designated as a university under the Act.

Subsequently the group notified the Institute of the criteria it intended to use in the assessment. It also requested that the main documentation (third submission) from the Institute, setting out how it already fulfilled these criteria or would fulfil them over time, be submitted in October 1997.

The review group would then visit the Institute in November 1997 before drafting its report.

The review group established the following criteria for the review and assessment of the Institute's application, within the overall context of the objects and functions of a university in sections 12 and 13 of the Universities Act:

- commitment to the advancement of knowledge through teaching, scholarship and research and an appropriate balance between each of the three activities
- provision of high quality programmes up to doctoral level, which are recognised both nationally and internationally and by the relevant professional bodies, as appropriate
- provision of an academic staff which has appropriate high level qualifications and professional standing in the community and among their peers
- provision of resources, both physical and financial, at a sufficiently high level to sustain the Institute's teaching and research activities on a continuing basis (in particular, the laboratory, library, information technology and lecturing facilities should be comparable to those in universities generally)
- a track record of producing graduates with high employability
- a demonstrated capacity to interact and collaborate with the various external communities and to thereby support and contribute to national economic and social development
- a mission statement and an ongoing strategic planning process to further advance the Institute's aims and objectives, including development plans that might enable it to meet all the criteria fully within a reasonable time.

The review group requested of the Institute that, in responding to each of the criteria set out, it incorporate the following specific information, with executive summaries provided where appropriate:

- a progress report on the implementation of the specific findings and recommendations of the 1996 report of the audit of quality assurance procedures in the Institute
- student numbers by faculty and course at each level, including validations by professional bodies
- graduate employment statistics by course
- numbers of academic and technical staff by grade and faculty
- academic qualifications, experience and scholarly and research interests of each academic staff member involved in third level work, by faculty, with details
- details of academic staff teaching hours per annum per student, length of academic year and the impact on the development of research
- staff training and development priorities and plans
- proposals for postgraduate programmes and research
- the multi-level nature of the DIT, its internal management and administration and plans for the non-third-level section of its activities
- liaison with business and industry and other external bodies
- physical facilities, existing provision and proposals for the future
- steps to reflect a university ethos, draft Charter and other measures.

Documentation submitted by the Institute

First submission to the review group

The first document submitted introduced in a preliminary way the core issue for the members of the review group. It presented the Institute's mission statement and a broad historical perspective of the Institute, including the partnership with the University of Dublin and the provisions of the DIT Act. It provided details on numbers of registered students and graduates at the different levels for the previous three academic years. It outlined the popularity of Institute courses on the Central Applications Office (CAO) system and the development of postgraduate research in the Institute, particularly since its formal establishment in 1993. It described the improving cohesion in the structures and practices across the Institute. It also summarised the institutional audit of quality assurance procedures carried out in the previous academic year, which led to the achievement of degree-awarding power. The document concluded by describing the con-straints which the DIT Act placed on the Institute's flexibility in manag-ing its day-to-day operations and the advantages of the greater autonomy which designation under the Universities Act would confer in this regard.

Second submission

At the request of the chairperson of the review group, the Institute submit-ted a second document in August 1997, detailing its case for designation as a university. In this document the main strands of the academic devel-opment of the Institute were repeated, the case was made that the Institute already functioned as a university, albeit as a multi-level one, and the general reasons for seeking designation as a university were set out. A further range of quantitative data about the Institute was also supplied in this submission.

In the general context of the Irish higher education system, the DIT had functioned effectively as a significant university level institution for up to twenty-five years. Under the partnership agreement with the Uni-versity of Dublin, primary degree awards of the university became avail-able to DIT graduates in nearly thirty diverse specialisms, leading to the award of 976 primary degrees in 1996.

The entry level of students on the Institute's degree courses compares favourably with a number of Irish universities and is significantly above that of the Regional Technical Colleges (RTCs), which are now regional Institutes of Technology (ITs). The range of minimum or cut-off points in the CAO system for entry into degree programmes for academic year 1996–1997, given in Table 6.1 for courses in the DIT and the other Irish institu-tions, indicates this.

Table 6.1: Minimum or cut-off points ranges for entry to higher education institutions 1996–1997

Cut-off Points Range	Institution
330 – 340	RTCs
370 – 380	Maynooth
400 – 410	UL, DIT
410 – 420	UCG, DCU
420 – 430	UCC
430 +	TCD, UCD

There is a substantial and growing involvement by all faculties of the Institute in programmes leading to primary degrees of the University of

Dublin. Table 8.2 gives the historical numbers of such graduates from the Institute, under the partnership agreement, each year since 1975.

Table 6.2 compares the Institute's output of primary degree graduates with those of the Irish universities for the six years 1993 to 1998.

Table 6.2: Numbers of primary degree graduates from the DIT, the Irish universities and all the institutions under the aegis of the NCEA in the six years 1993–1998						
	1993	1994	1995	1996	1997	1998
UCD	2,577	2,876	2,798	3,121	2,724	3,343
UCC	1,566	1,590	1,796	2,095	2,162	2,075
UCG	1,251	1,152	1,302	1,268	1,248	1,378
Maynooth	604	670	604	704	711	758
TCD*	1,560	1,913	1,798	2,014	2,063	2,195
DCU	624	665	670	1,448	1,628	1,754
UL	729	1,009	991	1,264	1,352	1,666
DIT	760	817	823	993	925	954
NCEA	991	1,243	1,573	2,077	2,349	3,140
(*Not including DIT graduates)						

Since 1994 there had been substantial development of taught postgraduate (postgraduate diploma and master's degree) programmes following the inclusion of the Institute within the nationally funded Advanced Technical Skills scheme. Until 1994 this scheme had applied to the universities only. The number of programmes sanctioned for the DIT within this scheme rose from one in 1994 to thirteen in 1997–98. The number of students graduating with taught postgraduate diplomas increased from forty in 1994–95 to 106 in 1995–96.

At the undergraduate level the Institute has a wide range of non-degree provision at certificate and diploma levels. Tables 8.3 and 8.4 list these programmes for all the faculty areas and as shown in Table 8.5, they produce over 2,000 graduates each year.

Demand for places on the Institute's degree courses is high with 6.6 per cent of all degree applicants making a DIT degree course their first choice in 1996 and 12.6 per cent doing so in 1999. Demand for non-degree courses in the Institute is very high with 39 per cent of the total first preferences within the CAO system being made to the DIT in 1996 and 25.6 per cent doing so in 1999.

The Institute's vision is that it will develop as a multi-level institution incorporating the best features of its educational past and enhancing the diversity now recognised as being vital in higher education. It will thus cater for all levels in higher education from apprentice to doctoral level. Given the technological emphasis of the Institute, it is important and appropriate that the ways in which the different levels are complementary to each other should be exploited. The changes occurring within apprenticeship in the recent past and the changes in many crafts due to developments in information and related technologies mean that the demarcation between craft-based technological and higher level activity will possibly converge in the years ahead. The Institute's policy of integrating craft activity into departments within its schools is likely to play a positive role in this regard.

The range of qualifications held by the staff of the Institute reflects its multi-level nature. In 1998 it had 687 academic staff working in its third level sector. Of these, ninety-five had doctorates, 227 master's degrees, 161 honours primary degrees and 204 other qualifications (mostly membership of professional bodies, which are all broadly equivalent to an honours primary degree). Some areas in the Institute, such as the faculty of science, have academic profiles more comparable with that of a traditional university. In other areas some 15 per cent of the staff have trade qualifications appropriate for teaching craft and apprentice courses.

The Institute has a strong commitment to the provision of opportunities for continuing staff development via funding for conferences and support for pursuing higher degrees through research and courses. It has devoted substantial and increasing funding to this activity in recent years — £0.5 million in 1995, £0.7 million in 1996 and £0.8 million in 1997.

The DIT has a strong and well-founded orientation to postgraduate research, as outlined in Chapter 9.

A multi-level higher education institution needs a suitable physical, social and intellectual environment in which students feel that they are at the centre of the community. It is widely acknowledged that the DIT provides high quality services that support students in their development in a caring environment, encouraging them to freely interact with staff. Students are involved in the decision-making processes at all levels in the Institute. The major weakness in the facilities of the DIT is undoubtedly its limited physical accommodation, situated on just over four hectares in total. Chapter 10 reviews this aspect of the Institute's profile and shows that in this respect the Institute is greatly under-resourced. However the hope is that the implementation of the Physical Development Plan, outlined in that chapter, will lead to very substantial developments in the coming years.

The courses and other programmes of the Institute have an applied emphasis, featuring extensive laboratory, studio and workshop activities and integrative project work, as well as study of the theoretical foundations. This educational philosophy has developed over many years of concerted quality improvement processes. The Institute is committed to developing this ethos.

A number of broad reasons were put forward as to why the Institute should be formally designated as a university.

In its academic work the Institute has to compete on many fronts with the universities and must provide courses, teaching, research and external collaborations of a quality and status comparable to those of the universities. It should not be constrained in its operating conditions in comparison to those given to the universities for comparable work, to enable it to attract good students and highly qualified staff in the years ahead. Designation as a university would enable DIT to engage on equal terms with universities to make more favourable contact with philanthropists and industrialists with a view to fundraising. This would in turn confirm the autonomy of the Institute and allow it to provide better services to students, graduates, staff and society in general.

Many of the reasons relating to institutional autonomy were articulated during the Oireachtas debates on the Universities Act. Mícheál Martin TD, Minister for Education and Science from 1997 to 2000, was opposition spokesperson on education when he said in Dáil Éireann on 12 March 1997,

> . . . The existing DIT Act has outlived its usefulness — it is far too restrictive on the DIT's capacity to grow and develop. It only allows for the appointment of staff subject to the approval of the Minister for Education with the concurrence of the Minister for Finance; the selection procedures for staff are determined by the Minister and the DIT; the appointment of research fellows, research assistants, etc. is subject to regulations laid down by the Minister for Education, again with the concurrence of the Minister for Finance; it can only charge fees for lectures, examinations and exhibitions subject to such conditions as may be specified by the Minister; it may only acquire land subject to the approval of the Minister; and so on. These provisions are not applicable to the universities. . . .

The Universities Act empowers a designated institution to manage its own affairs. It provides it with a suitable framework that allows for appropriate external representation on the governing body and a suitable level of institutional democracy and at the same time satisfying the State that there would be a proper balance between institutional autonomy and the needs of public policy and accountability.

Third submission

The main documentation (third submission) was submitted in late October 1997, after the review group had specified the criteria it intended to use in evaluating the Institute relative to Sections 12 and 13 of the Universities Act, and some additional quantitative data it required. The structure of this document followed closely the criteria set out by the review group. While much of the material in it had been covered in one or other of the earlier submissions, a number of significant additions were included.

The Institute provides a wide range of high quality programmes up to doctoral level and through its predecessor colleges, had demonstrated over a century of commitment to the advancement of knowledge.

The contract for lecturers stipulates a maximum of 560 timetabled hours per annum or an average of sixteen timetabled hours per week for thirty-five weeks. Teaching actually takes place over twenty-eight weeks a year, allowing some freedom for research activities in the rest of the year. Timetables can include a time allowance for the supervision of postgraduate students on the basis of two hours per week per student up to a four-hour maximum. Other allowances are also made.

While staff members have opportunities to become involved in research, nevertheless these opportunities need to be improved, particularly by creating an ethos which will encourage staff members to engage in research and providing better accommodation and facilities as well as increased time allocation.

The Institute had approximately 700 permanent or contract academic staff in 1997 involved in teaching at third level, 47 per cent of whom possessed master's degrees or doctoral qualifications.

In recent years the Institute provided substantial resources for staff development. Some thirty-two staff were studying for doctorates, seventy-eight for master's qualifications and twenty-seven for honours primary degrees.

The policy of the Institute in relation to recruitment has been, in practice, that new staff are only appointed if they possess a higher degree. Increasingly the higher qualification required (especially in certain discipline areas) is becoming a doctorate. By this means and through staff development there will soon be a significant enhancement of the academic profile, with over 25 per cent of staff members teaching on higher level programmes having PhDs and 50 per cent having master's degrees in the near future.

The complement of technical support staff within the Institute is lower than that pertaining in most universities. There are currently about 110 technical support staff distributed across the faculties. The deficiency in this area has been identified by the Institute in the Governing Body Report on Faculty Structures of May 1997 and a proposal has been put to the Department of Education for an additional eighty specialist technicians and laboratory aides.[7]

There are serious limitations on many of the Institute's facilities, including staff accommodation, space and resources for research and student social and sporting facilities, when the very large student population pursuing programmes of a diverse nature is considered. Nevertheless, the DIT has a long and distinguished record of producing graduates who have little difficulty in finding good employment in industry and the service sectors. It has developed myriad links to the outside world, both nationally and internationally. The most important links include those to the enterprise sector (mainly Irish-based), academic institutions, research centres at home and abroad and European Union (EU) programmes and projects. Included in the links to the enterprise sector are direct links to industries, professional bodies and institutions of state, including the semi-state sector. The international dimension of the Institute's activities includes participation in EU-funded projects together with partners from industry, European universities and state and professional bodies.

The first major strategic planning exercise in the newly independent Institute commenced in 1993 and focused on developing academic and management structures for the integrated Institute. The initial process, which led to the first faculty structure proposal in October 1994, revealed that a very substantial majority of staff felt it appropriate that the Institute should move towards a university-type structure while retaining the multi-level nature of the Institute. This transformation process is gradually underway.

The strategic planning process culminated in 1998 in the production by the Directorate of a discussion document on strategic issues, which includes a vision statement and aims for each key area of DIT activity. This document is undergoing extensive review by each faculty and the Governing Body. Arising from this review, the strategic plan for the Institute to the year 2010 will be formulated.

---

7.   *Faculty, School and Departmental Structures for the Dublin Institute of Technology*
     (Dublin: Dublin Institute of Technology), 1997.

Consultations of the review group

The review group visited the Institute in November 1997, met the Directorate, and toured a number of the research areas.

The group also consulted a wide number of relevant organisations and individuals — principally professional and educational — in coming to its conclusions. Twenty-four organisations responded, either in writing or orally. In early 1998, further views were solicited through advertisement in the national press and there were fourteen further respondents.

Most generally the feedback was favourable to the record of the Institute and to its designation as a university, provided this did not damage the Institute's ability to maintain and enhance its technician (diploma, certificate and apprenticeship) courses, i.e. its multi-level nature. The main educational respondents stressed the danger of mission drift in the Institute, possibly resulting in the depletion of technician level courses on which industry strongly depends.

In November 1997 the review group sought further clarifications on a number of issues. These included the question of mission or academic drift, the problems arising from the staff contract defining 20 June as the end of the academic year, alternative ways of improving the autonomy of the Institute and the development plans for the Academic Council, faculty structure, accommodation and academic profile of staff over the next five years or so. It also sought a brief historical review of the key stages in the academic evolution of the Institute.

Fourth submission

The fourth submission provided statements from the Institute on each of the issues raised in a letter from the review group. Most of these arguments had been put forward in various contexts in the earlier submissions.

This document reaffirmed the Institute's determination to develop its multi-level nature, firmly rooted in applied technological areas, and providing programmes leading to awards from apprentice level through certificate, diploma, primary degree and the highest postgraduate degrees.

It indicated how the staff contract is interpreted as flexibly as possible but how its basic structure is still determined by national agreements between the trade unions, the Department of Education and Science and the institutions.

It emphasised that the Academic Council remains the academic authority of the Institute under the DIT Act. In particular the Council is responsible for academic quality assurance and improvement at all levels.

The detailed plans for the faculty (and school) structure, agreed by Governing Body for the Institute, are now the subject of negotiations with the teachers' unions and the Department of Education and Science. In relation to physical developments, the second phase of the Aungier Street building was expected to begin soon and would eventually allow the consolidation of the faculty of business on that site, as part of the south city campus. The main physical developments hinge on the development of the Grangegorman site, which will allow the implementation of the Physical Development Plan over time. In relation to underpinning and helping to develop the research effort and, in turn, the academic profile in all faculties, it has been the plan to appoint senior research fellows in all faculties before 2000.

Comments on the approach of the review group

The conduct of the review was unsatisfactory in a number of ways, possibly reflecting the fact that it was the first time the process was carried out. The requests for submissions were in a piecemeal fashion as initially the HEA and later, the review group, felt their way through the process. Consequently there was an unnecessary amount of repetition in the documentary submissions from the Institute, a factor that possibly detracted from their impact. Also the interaction sought by the review group with the DIT was, in the main, through the president and a sub-group of the Directorate. The process differed quite considerably from the audit of quality assurance procedures two years previously (see Chapter 11). There was no broad participation or involvement within the Institute in the preparation and formulation of the documents submitted or in the overall review process. This is possibly one reason for an apparent lack of broad support among staff generally for the Institute's campaign for designation as a university. The process did not strongly relate or contribute to the development of team spirit or morale in the Institute. Indeed as a high level and generally opaque process, it may have been somewhat detrimental to institutional morale.

General comment on the Institute's application

As well as there being no internal explanatory campaign within the Institute during the immediate review process, it must also be acknowledged that there had been no documentation on the philosophical basis and values underpinning the operation and development of the Institute, in the academic press or in the Institute, in the years before the review. Historically the DIT and its predecessor colleges have tended to play a peripheral role in the educational debates in Ireland. Possibly conditioned by being under the aegis of the City of Dublin Vocational Education Committee and more recently under the direct control of the Department of Education and Science, this failure to engage in the more general processes of education has been a weakness in an institution as diverse as the DIT. Some individual staff members have participated in the debates down the years, but the Institute has not.

Consequently, neither the application for designation as a university, while a logical outcome of earlier developments and the emergence of the universities legislation, nor the arguments supporting that application, were well understood within the Institute or in the broad public arena.

REPORT OF THE REVIEW GROUP AND THE RESPONSE OF THE HEA

The report of the review group in 1998 located the Institute within the higher education sector in Ireland.[8] It reviewed the historical development and made a range of observations, academic evaluations and comments about the Institute and its operation. It also made a number of recommendations, many of which strongly echoed those of the review team two years before.

Specifically the report recommended that the DIT should be established as a university if and when a set of conditions is met. It set out the required conditions which referred to academic structures, collaboration with TCD, staff academic profile, quality assurance systems, development of non-degree courses, lifelong learning provision and the Institute's commitment to the preservation and development of its multi-level nature.

The review group further suggested that "detailed and costed plans with definitive targets for implementation should be drawn up by the DIT and agreed with the HEA" and that the "progress of the Institute towards these targets should be kept under ongoing review by the HEA in order to allow the Authority, when appropriate, to make its recommendations to Government in relation to the granting of university status to the Institute".

The HEA considered the report of the review group and, in forwarding

---

8. *Review of the Application by the Dublin Institute of Technology for Establishment as a University under Section 9 of the Universities Act (1997): Report of the International Review Group to the Higher Education Authority* (Dublin: Higher Education Authority), 1998.

it to the Minister for Education and Science in March 1999, commented on aspects of the report and added a number of further recommendations.[9]

The HEA accepted the advice of the group that the DIT should not be immediately established as a university. It considered as substantial the conditions set by the review group, of achieving adequate maturity and cohesiveness, appropriate staff and research profiles and academic structures. These challenges had indeed been highlighted in the report of the earlier review team in 1996.

The HEA made no comment on the report's evaluation of the DIT under the broad subjective and non-quantitative criteria derived from the Universities Act. However, the HEA took issue with the recommendation of the review group that the HEA itself would judge when the Institute had met the specified conditions to be established as a university and that these might reasonably be met within three to five years. Its view was that this envisaged a mentoring role for the HEA *vis-à-vis* the DIT and would require the DIT to be designated under the HEA Act in the near future and would also require a further review of the DIT after the three to five year period.

The HEA considered that the proposed mentoring role would constitute a confusion of its responsibilities. Such a role would be viewed as predetermining the final outcome. It could undermine the HEA's objectivity in relation to its final recommendation on the application of the DIT for designation as a university. It might erode the procedures set out in Section 9 of the Universities Act and diminish the standing of any institution successfully passing through these procedures for designation as a university. It is quite surprising that the review group should make recommendations that the HEA would find outside its remit. The HEA was represented on the review group and its report was available in draft to the HEA long before its publication.

In relation to the DIT being designated under the HEA Act, the HEA noted that any such designation would be under the provisions of the DIT Act, and that therefore it could not apply to the DIT "the same controls as it applies to institutions at present under its aegis". For instance issues of staffing and financial control for the DIT would continue as now and would not change to those set out in the Universities Act. The HEA was particularly concerned that such designation might be misinterpreted as an irrevocable stepping-stone to university designation. Again this was a sur-

9. *Recommendations of the Higher Education Authority to Government in Accordance with the Terms of Section 9 of the Universities Act 1997, Concerning the Application by DIT for Establishment as a University* (Dublin: Higher Education Authority), 1999.

prising concern, given that the proposal that DIT be designated under the HEA had first been made in the 1987 report on technological education of the International Study Group[10] and was announced as government policy in the 1995 White Paper.[11] Indeed in spring 2000, the Department of Education and Science is progressing the transfer of the DIT (and the other ITs) to the remit of the HEA.

In its other considerations, the HEA articulated the government's policy on maintaining the binary system in higher education. This was not a criterion set down for the Institute by the review group and it was not articulated in the relevant sections of the Universities Act.

The HEA decided that in the light of the three to five year period of development required by the DIT before it might be considered again for designation as a university, coupled with the significance of the conditions to be met by the Institute, a further review of the DIT would be required at that stage. The report of the HEA indicated that it would be inappropriate for the HEA itself to carry out this review, just as it would be inappropriate for it to mentor the Institute through the development and maturation process. Essentially the DIT would have to apply again to the Minister for Education and Science at the appropriate time for designation as a university under Section 9 of the Universities Act and the government would then decide whether to proceed with that process or not.

Summary

The DIT was already a major higher education institution with an impressive history when it was statutorily established in 1993. There followed a number of years of internal self-evaluation, planning and reorganisation. Initial steps in developing the management and administration for the new Institute were taken. The Academic Council was reorganised and quality assurance procedures were developed, systematised and implemented for undergraduate and postgraduate courses and postgraduate research work. The enhancement of the quality assurance procedures represented a deep institutional commitment to continuing improvement of standards and was based on devolving considerable autonomy to course committees and individual staff members.

This was generally a welcome change of culture across the Institute.

---

10. *Technological Education, Report of the International Study Group to the Minister for Education, op. cit.*
11. *Charting our Education Future, op. cit.*

However, change is not always congenial and the changes in the Institute occasionally led to concerns, uncertainty and disquiet. More than anything else it led to considerable intellectual ferment and possibly to an improved focussing on key academic issues and the interests of the students.

Not all the planned changes have yet been implemented. In particular the faculty structures are not in place and the challenge to relieve the shortage of physical accommodation still faces the Institute and its leadership. Thus the Institute is in a lengthy phase of change and is confronting the problems associated with the management of change.

The result of the quality audit of the Institute in 1996 was the gaining of degree-awarding power, the highest academic recognition ever achieved by the Institute.

In 1999, the outcome of the authoritative Section 9 evaluation of the Institute's case that it already fulfilled the objects and functions of a university as set out in the Universities Act, was that with a recommended process of improvement, the Institute could achieve designation as a university in three to five years. The report of the international review group of experts contained a considerable number of helpful and constructive suggestions for the elements of the strategic plan for the Institute to achieve such designation as a university within that time-frame.

However the HEA, in its response to this report, indicated that it could not mentor and monitor the process of improvement suggested by the review group. In that this Section 9 process was therefore completed, the HEA suggested that the Institute would need to undergo a new Section 9 process three to five years later.

Highlights of the DIT's Academic Profile

Chapter 7

Apprenticeship Education

During the first half of the twentieth century, the Dublin colleges, together with similar colleges in Cork and Limerick and a few other centres, developed a wide range of technical courses, mainly on a part-time basis, which were usually delivered in the evening. Comprehensive and innovative course provision and good standards were achieved even in the early years of the century.

The Dublin colleges pioneered apprenticeship education and such courses developed into the first systematic programmes with higher level components involving daytime attendance. Apprenticeship education became the broad foundation for the development of higher level work in technical, vocational and technological areas in the colleges, and indeed the foundation on which the Dublin Institute of Technology was built.

EARLY APPRENTICESHIP EDUCATION AND TRAINING

In the early 1900s, seminal developments within the Dublin colleges in the provision of part-time continuation education by day took place in the area of apprenticeship education. At the time there was no national scheme and the colleges developed schemes in collaboration with employers and trade organisations to facilitate and encourage apprenticeship. The colleges operated a competitive scholarship scheme and each year consulted with employers to decide the appropriate number of apprentice students to recruit and scholarships to offer. Each apprenticeship lasted for two years, thirty hours each week in the college, ten hours weekly of homework to be assessed and one month each year placement in the workshop of the employer. In 1926 there were 106 apprentice scholars in the Dublin colleges studying carpentry and joinery, cabinet making, electrical engineering, painting and decorating, motor car engineering, plumbing, printing, sheet metal work and quantity surveying.

DEVELOPMENTS UNDER THE APPRENTICESHIP ACT 1931

Following the Apprenticeship Act 1931, called for in the 1926 report of the Commission of Inquiry on Technical Education (see Chapter 3), which was designed "to make better provision for the regulation of apprenticeship in certain trades", the Minister for Industry and Commerce was empowered to declare a trade to be designated. This allowed relevant apprenticeship committees, including employer and employee representatives and ministerial nominees, to be set up to regulate the apprenticeship for those trades. They could not make it mandatory that an employer train and instruct an apprentice in a specific manner. Unfortunately, most trades did not adopt specific training and instruction schemes. Nevertheless, government bodies such as the Office of Public Works, semi-state bodies such as the Electricity Supply Board (ESB), the Irish Sugar Company and Córas Iompair Éireann (CIE), together with some private industries such as the Society of Irish Motor Traders and Arthur Guinness & Son, played a major role during the 1930s and 1940s in pioneering co-operative links which now are a common feature of apprenticeship and other educational work release schemes.

By the mid 1950s, there were 1,435 day release apprentices on training programmes distributed amongst the City of Dublin Vocational Education Committee (CDVEC) colleges and catering for the following trades:

• Bolton Street — printing, cabinet-making, motor, carpentry, CIE mechanical work

• Kevin Street — ESB electrician, ESB fitter, bakery, cinema projection

• Parnell Square — drapery, grocery, victualling, hairdressing

• Cathal Brugha Street — hotel and catering.

Day release varied from three hours to two and a half working days each week for the first two years of the apprenticeship. The CIE scheme was enlightened in that the apprentices were given a wider education, enabling some of them to advance to higher professional status. Most significant however, was the close association between the Dublin colleges and the industrial, trade and business life of the city.

Since the Dublin colleges pioneered apprenticeship education before the 1931 legislation, craft and apprenticeship activities were always a significant component of the work of the colleges and continue to be an important feature of the work of the DIT.

Until the 1960s the apprenticeship system was mainly a shared relationship between the employers and the colleges, as there was no industrial training authority in the country.[1] Employers were encouraged to re-lease their apprentices, first for a half-day and later a full day or more per week to attend the colleges and to sit for craft related examinations set by the Department of Education. This helped to raise the standards of crafts-manship in the country. But the effects were uneven geographically and tended to benefit industries that were already strong while leaving weak industries lagging behind.

APPRENTICESHIP EDUCATION UNDER THE APPRENTICESHIP ACT 1959

The Apprenticeship Act 1959 established the National Apprenticeship Board (An Cheard-Chomhairle) in 1960. It outlined day release and block release schemes for apprentice education. The Board was empowered to require all employers to send their apprentices to training courses in the colleges and technical schools. It also set the Day Vocational Certificate as the basic entry requirement. The Board specified the type of education and training for apprentices in the different trades and issued certificates at junior and senior level to successful apprentices. National apprentice-ship committees for the different designated trades were set up as well as local advisory groups.

In 1963 the Council for Education, Recruitment and Training for the Hotel Industry (CERT) was founded by the government to co-ordinate education and training with employers and the colleges, including appren-ticeship training, for the hospitality industry. This was not a designated trade, but the approach was similar to that of the National Apprenticeship Board for the engineering, technology and construction areas.

These schemes had a major impact on the apprentice education work of the Dublin colleges, especially those in Bolton Street, Kevin Street and Cathal Brugha Street. By 1965 the Dublin colleges had some 3,300 day release apprentices which was more than double the number of a decade before, and about 30 per cent of the national cohort. In Kevin Street alone the number of apprentices rose from some 300 in 1956 to over 1,100 in 1965.

In the elaboration of the Ballymun Project proposals, a key related plan was the development of the Bolton Street college as an apprentice education institute, gathering in apprenticeship activities in technological disciplines from the Kevin Street college.

---

1. P Gunnigle, N Heraty and M Morley, *Personnel and Human Resource Manage-ment: Theory and Practice in Ireland* (Dublin: Gill and Macmillan), 1997.

AN CHOMHAIRLE OILIÚNA (ANCO) AND RELATED DEVELOPMENTS

From the 1960s to the 1980s apprenticeship education and training underwent a significant change after the Apprenticeship Act 1959. The reorganisation of the Government's involvement continued with the enactment of the Industrial Training Act 1967 which led to the setting up of a
new national training authority, An Chomhairle Oiliúna (AnCO). AnCO
was to play an active role in reforming the apprenticeship system and
regulating entry to different designated trade areas.

By the 1970s the Dublin colleges had considerable involvement in
apprentice training and in 1976 the Apprentice Education Board was established within the DIT by the CDVEC to co-ordinate the activities in
this area. At the time there were widespread concerns about the potential
shortages of craftspersons for different trades. In the 1980s AnCO received extensive European Community funding and established a number
of its own well equipped training centres to engage in extensive training
activities, part of which duplicated the work of the DIT in relation to apprenticeship.

The colleges of the DIT continued to provide courses for apprentices
attending through block release or day release arrangements and special
efforts were made to eliminate duplication of efforts between the education and AnCO sectors. The relationship between the colleges and AnCO
was essentially one in which the colleges provided an educational and
training service as specified by AnCO as a client. However there was also
considerable co-operation between DIT staff (generally in conjunction
with the Apprentice Education Board) and AnCO in relation to up-dating
and developing syllabuses and the co-ordination of work-release arrangements.

APPRENTICE EDUCATION BOARD

In 1976 the CDVEC established the Apprentice Education (Industrial
Crafts) Board to advise on matters of policy regarding apprentice education with particular reference to:

• co-ordination and development of courses

• the relationship with AnCO and other external bodies.

The board was to be chaired by the head of the School of Trades in the
Bolton Street college and the membership would include the department
heads in building trades, metal fabrication, auto engineering, aero-engi-

neering, engineering trades, electrical installation, cookery, waiting, bakery, and printing. The principals in the Kevin Street and Bolton Street colleges also nominated members. Later, elected staff representatives became members of the board.

Initially the board reported to the CDVEC but, after the establishment of the DIT and its Governing Body in 1978, the board reported to the Governing Body.

The Apprentice Education Board was responsible for validating all trade and trade related courses in the Institute. In conjunction with course advisory committees, the board organised the continuous review of courses as changes happened in work practices, materials, products and industrial technology. It co-ordinated the arrangements for educational release of apprentices in liaison with other educational institutions, the training agencies and external training centres.

Broadly the Apprentice Education Board functioned in parallel with the Academic Council, the former relating to apprenticeship courses and the latter to general third level courses.

With the statutory establishment of the DIT in 1993, the Apprentice Education Board was fully incorporated within the Academic Council as the Apprentice Education Committee with specific terms of reference relating to the education, training and employment of apprentices.

REFORM OF APPRENTICESHIPS UNDER FORAS ÁISEANNA SAOTHAIR (FÁS)

Under the provisions of the Labour Services Act 1987 AnCO was reconstituted by the new Department of Labour into a new Government agency, Foras Áiseanna Saothair (FÁS), with a wider remit relating to manpower services.

As part of the Government's national programme in 1991 it was decided to establish a new standards-based apprenticeship for the twenty-six designated trades, which would have three main features as follows:

• standards-based — for successful completion of the apprenticeship and the award of a national craft qualification, the apprentice must achieve pre-set standards of skill and knowledge

• modular in structure with alternating phases of training on-the-job with the employer and off-the-job in a FÁS training centre or educational institution

• the national qualification as a compulsory requirement for recognition as a craftsperson by employers or trade unions.

FÁS was given the leading role in structuring and implementing the new system. The Department of Education, the DIT, the Regional Technical Colleges, employers and trade unions also engaged in a series of tripartite committees dealing with the different trades.

The new system began its implementation stage in 1993. The DIT colleges in Bolton Street and Kevin Street are involved in the following trade areas: construction plant fitter; heavy vehicle mechanic; toolmaker; metal fabricator; plumber; bookbinder; carton maker; originator; printer; bricklayer; cabinet maker; painter/decorator; plasterer; wood machinist; aircraft mechanic; refrigeration craftsperson; sheet metal worker; vehicle body repairer; carpentry and joinery; fitting; motor mechanic; electrician and instrumentation.

Under the most recent arrangements, each apprentice's overall three year programme will be divided into seven phases. Phases 1, 3, 5 and 7 will be "on the job" in the apprentice's place of employment and phases 2, 4 and 6 "off the job", generally attending a FÁS training centre for phase 2 and college (including the DIT) for phases 4 and 6. Typically phase 2 extends over twenty weeks of full-time attendance and phases 4 and 6 are each of ten weeks duration, although there are likely to be some variations in the arrangements depending on the trade specialisation.

The assessment arrangements leading to the award of national craft qualifications are still under discussion but it seems likely that they will be issued under the aegis of the proposed National Qualifications Authority.[2] This new authority is planned to be an umbrella organisation co-ordinating the work of the new Further Education and Training Awards Council. This in turn will make appropriate awards, replacing those now made by the NCEA, the National Council for Vocational Awards (NCVA) and other bodies such as FÁS, Teagasc and CERT.

In this changing situation, some of the DIT schools are still involved in offering day release courses for apprentices in non-designated trades and crafts, who continue to prepare for City and Guilds of London Institute and national examinations and awards. It is likely that these programmes will be phased out in the coming years and converted to programmes leading to awards under the proposed National Qualifications Authority.

The new apprenticeship scheme was envisaged as having a national intake of 3,500 young people each year, giving a total apprentice population of over 10,000 at any one time. With the recent improvement in the

---

2.   *Qualifications (Education and Training) Act* (Baile Átha Cliath: Oifig an tSoláthair), 1999.

economy, this figure has reached over 16,000 during the 1998–1999 academic year. There are now more apprentices registered than at any time since the early 1980s and since 1996 there are more than 4,000 new candidates registering for apprenticeship programmes annually. Table 8.6 gives the apprentice enrolments in the DIT since 1982. By the early 1990s the DIT catered for some 40 per cent of the national apprentice population and if this percentage is maintained, the Institute is expected to have some 5,000 to 6,000 apprentices enrolled in the years ahead. Based on their time in the Institute and their corresponding study load, the number of apprentices attending on a part-time basis corresponds to an equivalent full-time student number of up to 2,000.

In order to underpin the Institute's commitment to a continuing significant role in apprentice education, the policy is to integrate craft apprentice activity into departments within related schools in the proposed faculty structures.

The Scientific and Technological Investment Education fund launched in 1997 afforded £10 million in funding to the Institutes of Technology for the provision of extra places on phases 4 and 6 of apprenticeship training programmes. While some of the Institutes of Technology have benefited significantly from this funding, the DIT has been unable to benefit to the same extent because of limitations on the physical expansion possible in the trade areas of the Institute. The development of the new campus at Grangegorman should allow this expansion in the early years of this decade. With the construction, engineering, food and tourism industries now growing at an unprecedented rate in Ireland, it is safe to predict that extra skilled craftspeople will be needed over that decade.

SUMMARY

In the newly independent Saorstát Éireann, the Dublin colleges helped to shape the Vocational Education Act 1930 and then proceeded to steadily plan and develop their services within the CDVEC, under the aegis of that legislation. Under the different Apprenticeship Acts and the national systems established, the colleges contributed to the provision of the educational elements of apprenticeship training in a wide range of disciplines.

This will continue and apprenticeship programmes will be an important and developing aspect of the multi-level nature of the Institute.

Chapter 8

Higher Level Courses in the Institute

Third-level or higher education courses offered on a part-time, evening basis have been a significant feature of the Dublin colleges since the early years of this century.

FULL-TIME HIGHER LEVEL COURSES

The laboratory and technical facilities developed during the 1940s and 1950s for the range of apprenticeship courses and the experience gained by the staff in delivering these practical programmes helped to lay the foundation for the more specialised post-apprenticeship technician and technological programmes that were established during the 1960s. Initially these involved part-time attendance (day as well as evening) and later developed into the full-time courses, which were subsequently developed by the Technical Institute in Bolton Street and the Institute of Science and Technology in Kevin Street.

After the Second World War, as the demands for technological and commercial expertise grew in the Irish economy, enrolments in higher level courses in the Dublin colleges expanded rapidly. These were accommodated by transferring out some of the junior work to new second-level CDVEC schools which had been built in various parts of the city and suburbs and by providing extensions to the colleges or otherwise acquiring some additional accommodation for them. New higher grades of specialist higher technological full-time posts for teachers were created and a number of full-time post-Leaving Certificate courses were developed in the Kevin Street, Bolton Street and Rathmines colleges in response to growing demands from students and the encouragement of employers and professional bodies. Many of the courses catered for discipline areas that were not otherwise provided for in the Republic of Ireland's (as Saorstát Éireann had become in 1949) higher education system.

Initially the primary objective of these full-time courses was to assist students to prepare for the examinations of the appropriate professional bodies, for instance in accounting, architecture and engineering, and for the external examinations of London University. Soon they were broadened to include additional academic subjects and practical laboratory and project work. The next development, essential in assuring standards, was that the students were required to take college examinations in addition to those of the professional or external bodies and these were used to determine their progress from one year of a course to the next. Where students were successful in the college examinations they were awarded college diplomas, in addition to the awards of the appropriate external bodies that they would receive upon successful completion of the external examinations.

In general these professional (usually at primary degree level) and technological (subdegree level) courses were offered in full-time, part-time day, part-time evening, and sandwich modes. For instance the architecture course was full-time for three years and on a sandwich basis for a further two. At the end of the fifth year the students took the final examinations of the Royal Institute of Architects of Ireland. An alternative part-time route to the same examination was also provided. In mechanical engineering a four-year course offered on a sandwich basis led to the examinations of the Institution of Mechanical Engineers.

With the help of discipline advisory committees consisting of representatives of employers, professional bodies and trade unions, the technological courses were organised as closely analogous to the professional courses and generally achieved some level of recognition by the professional bodies, such as partial remission in the requirements for membership. By the mid-1950s higher level courses in the Dublin colleges covered the following areas:

- Bolton Street — architecture, quantity surveying, building surveying, valuation surveying, land surveying, building technology, mechanical engineering, motor car engineering, marine engineering, aeronautical engineering, heating, ventilating and air conditioning
- Kevin Street — electrical engineering, radio engineering, applied science, air navigation, food, water and drug analysis, industrial microbiology and optometry
- Rathmines college – business
- Cathal Brugha Street – hotel and catering.

Typically, the professional bodies determined and issued their own syllabuses and administered the appropriate examinations. The Dublin colleges provided the courses, often on a part-time basis, to prepare the students for these professional examinations. In this way, the colleges provided valuable opportunities for many young people to prepare for technical and professional careers, at a time when full-time third level education was available to only a small minority of the Irish population.

HIGHER TECHNICIAN PROGRAMMES

The development of the Irish economy in the 1960s led to a demand for high quality technicians and other specialist personnel in various discipline areas. These needs were highlighted in two reports sponsored by the Organisation for Economic Co-operation and Development (OECD), one in 1962 on issues relating to the funding of education,[1] and the second in 1964 on technician training in Ireland.[2] The Dublin colleges responded by developing a number of new full-time technician programmes which were specifically designed to address needs identified in those reports, generally in consultation with representatives of industry and commerce. In some cases they paralleled and complemented the other full-time courses being offered, which were geared towards the membership requirements of different professional bodies and had been developed over the previous decade. Both sets of courses frequently drew on the same staff expertise and physical resources.

PROFESSIONAL AND DEGREE-LEVEL PROGRAMMES

By the early 1960s the colleges had successfully operated a range of full-time courses leading to college diploma awards. Furthermore, they had employed distinguished external experts as course development advisers and external examiners for monitoring and assuring standards in these courses. As a result a number of the professional bodies accepted the relevant college diplomas as fully meeting their academic requirements for corporate membership. In areas such as engineering, the college diploma was thus accorded the same recognition as a primary degree award from a university. This development also led to the acceptance of these diplomas as meeting the requirements for entry into postgraduate work in universities in Ireland (particularly TCD) and abroad.

---

1.   *Investment in Education, op. cit.*
2.   *Training of Technicians in Ireland, op. cit.*

DEVELOPMENT OF COURSES UNDER THE PARTNERSHIP AGREEMENT

A full listing of DIT courses, which were approved by the University under the terms of the partnership agreement between the DIT and the University of Dublin, is given in Table 8.1. The years when each degree course was first approved are also listed.

This table demonstrates the sustained high level academic development and achievement from 1975 to the present. Beginning in the engineering and built environment areas, it soon involved all the main discipline areas and colleges of the DIT, where earlier apprentice developments and then certificate and diploma level programmes had been successfully developed.

All of these courses attracted diploma awards of the Institute and parallel degree awards from the University of Dublin under the partnership agreement and will continue to do so until 2002 or 2003.

Table 8.1 Courses in CDVEC/DIT recognised for degree awards by University of Dublin/Trinity College Dublin (TCD)

Course	College*	University degree	Year approved
(a) Applied arts			
Diploma in Music Education	(Ad)	BMusEd	1985
(joint course between DIT, TCD and RIAM)			
Graduate Diploma in Music Performance	(Ad)	BMus (Perf)	1991
Advanced Diploma in Communications			
(Film/Broadcasting)	(A)	BSc (Media)	1992
(Journalism)	(A)	BSc (Media)	1995
Diploma in Management Law (part-time)	(A)	BSc (Mgmt)	1990
(b) Built environment			
Diploma in Property Economics			
(Valuation/Surveying)	(B)	BSc (Surv)	1977
Diploma in Construction Economics			
(Quantity Surveying)	(B)	BSc (Surv)	1977
Diploma in Architecture	(B)	BSc (Arch)	1977
Diploma in Construction Economics (part-time)			
(Quantity Surveying)	(B)	BSc (Surv)	1977
(c) Business			
Advanced Diploma in Marketing Techniques	(M)	BSc (Mgmt)	1977
Diploma in Advanced Business Studies	(A)	BSc (Mgmt)	1977
Advanced Diploma in Administration/Marketing	(M)	BSc (Mgmt)	1995
Diploma in Management Services (part-time)	(A)	BSc (Mgmt)	1994
Diploma in Health Services Management			
(part-time)	(A)	BSc (Mgmt)	1996

Course	College*	University degree	Year approved
(d) Engineering			
Diploma in Engineering			
(Electrical/Electronic) *(Original single option)*	(K)	BSc (Eng)	1975
(Mechanical)	(B)	BSc (Eng)	1975
(Structural)	(B)	BSc (Eng)	1976
(Manufacturing)	(B)	BSc (Eng)	1977
(Electrical Power)	(K)	BSc (Eng)	1983
(Control Systems)	(K)	BSc (Eng)	1983
(Communication Systems)	(K)	BSc (Eng)	1983
(Building Services)	(B)	BSc (Eng)	1983
Diploma in Engineering (part-time)			
(Mechanical)	(B)	BSc (Eng)	1975
(Structural)	(B)	BSc (Eng)	1976
(Manufacturing)	(B)	BSc (Eng)	1977
(Building Services)	(B)	BSc (Eng)	1983
(e) Science			
Diploma in Applied Sciences			
(Physics/Chemistry)	(K)	BSc (AppSc)	1977
(Physics /Mathematics)	(K)	BSc (AppSc)	1977
(Chemistry/Mathematics)	(K)	BSc (AppSc)	1977
(Physics/Computer Science)	(K)	BSc (AppSc)	1989
(Mathematics/Computer Science)	(K)	BSc (AppSc)	1989
(Food Science/Food Technology)	(K)	BSc (AppSc)	1989
(Computer Science/Software Engineering)	(K)	BSc (AppSc)	1990
Diploma in Human Nutrition and Dietetics	(K)	BSc (HN&D)	1982
(joint course between DIT and TCD)			
Diploma in Biomedical Sciences	(K)	BSc (AppSc)	1990
(f) Tourism and food			
Diploma in Environmental Health	(C)	BSc (EnvH)	1984
Higher Diploma in Hotel/Catering Management	(C)	BSc (Mgmt)	1977

*A denotes Aungier Street/Rathmines; Ad, Adelaide Road; B, Bolton Street; C, Cathal Brugha Street; K, Kevin Street; M, Mountjoy Square.

To further illustrate the magnitude of this academic achievement across the Institute, Table 8.2 gives the numbers of graduates classified by discipline area who, having received DIT diploma awards, also became eligible for appropriate degree awards of the University since 1975. It can be seen from this table that in 1975, a total of twenty-eight engineering graduates from Bolton Street and Kevin Street became eligible for degree awards. In 1977, when architecture, surveying, business studies and marketing were included, the number of graduates eligible for degree awards increased to 134. In 1980, with the inclusion of applied sciences, the number

Table 8.2: Numbers of DIT graduates (by course and year) who also became eligible for degree awards of the University under the terms of the Partnership Agreement

	Applied Arts				Built Environment			Business					Engineering					Science			Food		
Year	Music Perf	Music Ed	Comm	Mgmt Law	Arch	Constr Econ	Prop Econ	Bus Studies	Market	Admin/ Market	Health Mgmt	Mgmt Serv	Elect	Mech	Struc	Prod Man	Bldg Serv	Appl Sci	Human Nutrit	Biomed Sci	Hotel & Cater	Environ Health	Totals
1975													10	18									28
1976													9	16	6								31
1977					42	27	11	7	13				14	5	11	4							134
1978					49	20	19	10	19				15	11	20	3					6		172
1979					25	19	19	18	18				16	5	21	5					7		153
1980					20	20	15	6	19				25	14	13	14		11			15		172
1981					39	26	17	25	26				25	23	19	23		13			8		244
1982					26	26	7	20	29				26	15	14			22			16		201
1983					26	26	15	31	32				44	22	20	5		28			16		265
1984					21	46	17	16	38				40	19	22	11		22			22		274
1985					31	39	15	81	62				34	21	30	12		28			18		371
1986					41	44	23	52	81				70	29	21	14	13	35	11		37	20	491
1987					27	50	14	68	108				65	30	16	17	14	45	13		40	23	530
1988					28	45	23	66	62				56	33	27	17	13	43	14		34	22	483
1989					22	41	17	69	89				54	25	28	19	16	60	15		35	20	510
1990		3			22	57	27	91	100				72	26	19	12	17	35	17		39	21	558
1991	8				27	46	32	80	112				53	34	21	22	23	36	18		19	49	580
1992	2				33	38	21	97	91				61	32	23	25	21	50	21	39	42	10	606
1993	2	5	21		30	57	41	90	110				72	41	32	17	22	64	21	32	43	60	760
1994	2		24	47	34	64	36	87	109				60	40	38	18	22	114	14	28	54	26	817
1995	12	7	21	44	35	59	36	90	100				67	39	27	24	20	87	21	30	68	36	823
1996	8	3	24	51	47	61	44	100	141	58			72	25	42	23	17	126	19	27	52	36	976
1997	6		41	43	53	48	36	80	109	63			44	42	26	22	24	125	26	35	51	30	904
1998	6	4	26	49	65	39	40	76	101	58	35	20	56	51	46	22	25	124	20	33	54	31	981
1999	11		45	21	29	35	51	106	112	69	24	23	78	44	33	22	21	89	21	33	62	31	960
Total	57	22	202	255	772	933	576	1366	1681	248	59	43	1138	660	575	351	268	1157	251	257	738	415	12024

had risen to 172. By 1989 environmental health and human nutrition and dietetics had been added and with increased outputs from other courses there were 510 eligible graduates, and in 1999 the number of DIT graduates eligible for degree awards of the University was 936. The growth in the numbers since 1990 has been due more to significantly increased enrolments in existing approved courses than to large increases in the total number of approved courses.

OTHER HIGHER LEVEL COURSES OFFERED BY THE INSTITUTE

Other courses leading to primary degree awards of the Institute itself, offered across the Institute in the academic year 1999/2000, are listed in Table 8.3.

Table 8.3: Course in the Institute leading to primary degree awards of the Institute itself in academic year 1999/2000	
Course Title	**College**
(a) Applied arts	
Printing Management	(B)
International Business/Languages (French)	(K)
International Business/Languages (German)	(K)
International Business/Languages (Spanish)	(K)
International Business/Languages (English)	(K)
Photography	(TB*)
Social Care	(R**)
Early Childhood Care/Education	(R)
Design (Interior and Furniture)	(M)
Design (Visual Communication)	(M)
Fine Art	(M)
(* Temple Bar)	
(** Rathmines)	
(b) Built Environment	
Geomatics	(B)
(c) Business	
Business Information Systems Development	(A)
Retail and Services Management	(M)
(d) Engineering	
Transport Technology	(B)
Electrical Engineering	(K)
(d) Science	
Optometry	(K)
Chemical Sciences	(K)
Applied Sciences (Biochemistry/Molecular Biology)	(K)
Mathematics	(K)

Course Title	College
(e) Tourism and Food	
Tourism Marketing	(C)
Culinary Arts	(C)
Leisure Management	(C)
(colleges as Table 8.1)	

Table 8.4: Full-time diploma and certificate courses offered in the Institute, grouped according to faculty, in academic year 1999/2000

Course Title	College
(a) Applied arts	
Certificate In Design (Display)	(M)
Certificate in Design (Presentation)	(M)
Certificate in Media Production	(M)
Diploma in Music Teaching	(Ad)
Diploma in Speech/Drama Studies	(Ad)
(b) Built environment	
Diploma in Architectural Technology	(B)
Certificate/Diploma in Construction Technology	(B)
Certificate/Diploma in Auctioneering/Valuation/Estate Agency	(B)
Certificate in Buildings Maintenance	(B)
Diploma in Environmental Resources Management	(B)
(c) Business	
Certificate in Transport Management	(A)
Professional Accountancy*	(A)
Certificate in Business Studies	(A)
Certificate/Diploma in Marketing	(M)
Certificate in Business Studies (Management)	(M)
Certificate in Business Studies (Retail Marketing)	(M)
Certificate in Business Studies (Proprietorship)	(M)
Certificate in Business Studies (Security)	(M)
(*external award)	
(d) Engineering	
Certificate/Diploma in Civil Engineering	(B)
Certificate/Diploma in Building Services Engineering	(B)
Certificate/Diploma in Mechanical Engineering	(B)
Certificate/Diploma in Transport Engineering/Management	(B)
Diploma in Electrical/Control Engineering	(K)
Certificate in Electrical/Electronic Drafting	(K)
Certificate/Diploma in Industrial Electronic Systems	(K)
Diploma in Applied Electronics	(K)
Certificate in Electronics	(K)

Course Title	College
(e) Science	
Certificate in Medical Laboratory Sciences	(K)
Diploma in Computer Science	(K)
Diploma in Applied Science (Applied Biology)	(K)
Diploma in Applied Science (Applied Chemistry)	(K)
Diploma in Applied Science (Applied Physics)	(K)
Diploma of the Institute of Food Science and Technology*	(K)
(*external award)	
(f) Tourism and food	
Diploma in Baking Technology/Management	(K)
Diploma in Hotel/Catering Management	(C)
Certificate in Travel/Tourism	(C)
Certificate in Hotel/Catering Supervision	(C)
Certificate in Culinary Arts (Professional Chef)	(C)
Certificate/Diploma in Food Technology	(C)
Certificate/Diploma in Food Quality Assurance (Horticulture)	(C)
Certificate/Diploma in Health Care Technology	(C)
Certificate in Business Studies (Meat Management)	(M)
Certificate in Business Studies (Bar Management)	(M)
(colleges as Table 8.1)	

In addition to degree level courses, the wide range of three-year full-time diploma courses and two-year full-time certificate courses listed in Table 8.4 are offered across the faculties of the Institute. In the chronology of the emergence of these courses, the early origins of some of them are in the 1960s and even earlier. The table shows the involvement of schools across the Institute in these higher level courses, which mostly grew organically from earlier vocational and apprentice programmes and courses that prepared students for external examinations of professional bodies.

Table 8.4 adds to the picture developed in the previous three tables of sustained academic development, achievement and service by all the discipline areas of the Institute since the 1960s.

The Institute gives a high priority to developing postgraduate research (see Chapter 9) and provides a range of postgraduate courses. Table 8.5 lists the twenty-eight such courses offered on a full-time or part-time in the academic year 1999/2000.

Table 8.5 Postgraduate diploma (PgDip) and master's degree (MA or MSc) courses offered, grouped according to faculty, in academic year 1999/2000

Course Title	College
(a) Applied arts	
PgDip/MA in Interactive Media	(A)
PgDip/MA in Music Technology	(Ad)
PgDip/MA in Public Relations	(A)
PgDip/MA in Journalism	(A)
PgDip/MA in Film Production	(A)
PgDip/MA in Media Studies	(A)
PgDip/MA in Design in Digital Media	(A)
PgDip in Criminological Studies	(A)
(b) Built Environment	
PgDip/MSc in Regional/Local Development	(B)
PgDip/MSc in Sustainable Development	(B)
PgDip/MSc in Planning and Development	(B)
(c) Business	
PgDip/MSc in Marketing (Business to Business)	(M)
PgDip/MSc in Marketing (International)	(M)
PgDip/MSc in Marketing (Direct Marketing)	(M)
PgDip/MSc in Marketing (Services Marketing)	(M)
PgDip in Internet Systems Development	(M)
PgDip in Accounting	(A)
PgDip/MSc in Advertising	(A)
(d) Engineering	
PgDip/MSc in Information Technology Engineering	(B)
PgDip/MSc in Applied Computing for Technologists	(B)
PgDip/MSc in Engineering Computation	(B)
(e) Science	
PgDip/MSc in Computing (Strategic Management)	(K)
PgDip/MSc in Computing (Distributed Systems)	(K)
PgDip/MSc in Molecular Pathology*	(K)
PgDip/MSc in Pharmaceutical Quality Assurance	(K)
(*jointly with the University of Dublin)	
(f) Tourism and Food	
PgDip/MSc in Tourism Management	(C)
PgDip/MSc in Hospitality Management	(C)
PgDip/MSc in Environmental Health Risk Management	(C)

(colleges as Table 8.1)

COURSES VALIDATED IN EXTERNAL ORGANISATIONS

The DIT is committed to working in partnership with appropriate external organisations and institutions in Ireland and abroad because of the mutual benefits which can arise from collaborative programmes of study and, more importantly, the increased opportunities such provision makes available to a wide range of students. The forms of collaboration include the validation and franchising of programmes of study and joint courses and awards. Currently the Institute has partnerships with the Electricity Supply Board (ESB) and Radio Telefís Éireann (RTÉ), and RESPOND, a voluntary housing organisation where these organisations provide courses for their staff which lead to awards of the DIT. In the case of the ESB there is a certificate courses for power plant operators and managers and in the case of RTÉ there is a postgraduate diploma/MA in broadcasting (television operations). The organisations involved and the staff and community who benefit from the scheme value the courses as part of their staff development programmes.

CHANGES IN ENROLMENTS OVER THE YEARS

In 1961 the full-time population of the Dublin colleges was close to 4,400, of which 15 per cent were higher level students and the rest second level continuation education students. There were, however, also some 19,500 part-time, mostly evening students and some 2,200 apprentices. By the end of the 1970s most of the continuation education work had been distributed to second level schools in the CDVEC system and the full-time population in the DIT colleges was about 3,500. With the national expansion of higher education, the part-time student numbers had dropped to about 9,500 but apprentice numbers had grown to 6,200.

Table 8.6 gives the historical enrolments of full-time higher level, part-time and apprenticeship students in the Institute since 1982.

The full-time student population of the DIT almost doubled between 1982 and 1993, with the rate of growth in enrolments being highest in the late 1980s and early 1990s. Apprentice numbers fluctuated in accordance with the buoyancy of the economy and, to an extent, with the manner in which apprenticeship was promoted by AnCO and latterly by FÁS. Part-time student enrolments remained significant but showed a general downward trend during the late 1980s and early 1990s.

These numbers do not include the thousands of participants in short courses throughout the Institute.

Table 8.6: Total annual DIT enrolments since 1982			
Year	**Full-time**	**Part-time**	**Apprentices**
1982–83	4,937	11,187	7,343
1983–84	5,428	10,663	6,744
1984–85	5,892	10,798	5,923
1985–86	6,175	10,479	5,259
1986–87	6,333	9,909	4,825
1987–88	6,679	9,680	4,568
1989–90	7,132	9,960	4,567
1990–91	7,997	9,878	5,412
1991–92	9,139	9,818	5,509
1992–93	9,299	9,551	5,192
1993–94	9,815	8,787	4,929
1994–95	9,649	8,553	4,201
1995–96	9,933	7,956	3,649
1996–97	10,247	7,183	3,524
1997–98	9,990	7,796	2,988
1998–99	9,863	8,006	2,870

SUMMARY

Before the Vocational Education Act 1930, the Dublin colleges offered an appreciable number of part-time higher level courses. In the 1930s the CDVEC developed the earliest plans for a higher education Institute in the centre of Dublin. At that early stage the principles underpinning these plans included autonomy and the power to grant diploma awards, clear differentiation between higher level and second level work, an applied orientation, links with the professional bodies and with industry and commerce, qualified teachers and research.

The early 1960s heralded the beginnings of the modern expansion in higher education in Ireland, strongly supported by government policies and funding. Each of the Dublin colleges under the aegis of the CDVEC contributed to providing higher level courses to meet the demand from increasing numbers of students.

The partnership with the University of Dublin offered a welcome solution to the pressing need for additional degree places in Irish higher education in the 1970s, 1980s and 1990s

Currently the DIT is the largest higher education institution in the State in terms of total student numbers. In this respect it is larger than University College Dublin, the largest university. The full-time equivalent enrolment, of over 12,000, has 4 per cent postgraduate, 38 per cent primary degree, 24 per cent diploma, 24 per cent certificate and 10 per cent apprenticeship students. The DIT is thus a thoroughly multi-level institution, offering opportunities for able students to progress vertically in most discipline areas to the highest academic level.

Chapter 9

Postgraduate Research

The evolving nature of the activities of the colleges of the Dublin Institute of Technology presented them with increasing problems in the 1980s as they sought to operate as effectively as possible as higher level institutions. These problems arose mainly from the restrictions imposed by the Vocational Education Act 1930, which was primarily intended to encompass a second-level education provision. As the Institute began to engage in research and development work, difficulties arose.[1] These restrictions may be seen in bolder relief when one considers the broad academic maturity that had been achieved by the Institute and its colleges at that stage.

DEVELOPMENT OF RESEARCH ACTIVITIES IN THE INSTITUTE

The International Study Group on technological education, in its report to the Minister for Education in 1987, stated that it "was impressed by the work of the colleges" and recognised "the high standing which the colleges hold in their special fields of study".[2] It went on to state that the "research activities of the DIT are wide ranging, as would be expected in an Institute of such diverse character. Collaboration with other researchers and institutions both nationally and internationally is a common feature of much research carried out by the Institute." This report recommended that statutory provision be made for the Institute to engage in this type of work and that it should be encouraged to make its expertise and facilities more widely available to industry and business as considered appropriate.

Over the years, priority had been given in recruitment in most areas to established professionals in their specialist disciplines. Many of the Institute's permanent academic staff had availed of the opportunities to enhance their qualifications since their recruitment and were involved in

---

1. *Barriers to Research and Development in the Higher Education Sector, op. cit.*
2. *Technological Education, Report of the International Study Group to the Minister for Education, op. cit.*

research or consultancy work appropriate to their discipline areas.

Statutory provision was made in the DIT Act 1992 for the Institute to engage in research, consultancy and development work, either on its own or with other institutions, and to provide services in relation to such work and enter into arrangements, including participation in limited companies, to exploit the results of this work.

RESEARCH WITHIN THE INSTITUTE

The Institute undertook to develop the postgraduate research aspect of its work in a more focussed manner after the DIT Act 1992 was implemented in 1993.

Research work, leading to the advancement of knowledge, is recognized as a necessary element for underpinning education, whether at postgraduate or undergraduate level, and to help ensure a lifelong learning approach to knowledge and skills. It is a key element of the Institute's mission.

Postgraduate research and development projects may be carried out in the wide areas of scholarship in which the Institute has relevant expertise. These involve areas of scientific, commercial, industrial, social, professional and artistic scholarship, as well as educational matters and academic management and administration. Interdisciplinary work and collaborative research projects with other educational, research, industrial, commercial, professional or governmental organizations in Ireland, in the European Union (EU) and further afield, are especially encouraged.

The development of postgraduate research activities in the Institute is encouraged because of their strong role in helping to maintain the standard, quality and relevance of the undergraduate and postgraduate courses offered. Research, development and consultancy work is therefore viewed as essential in underpinning the key teaching functions of the Institute at all levels.

Research activities had been promoted positively by the Institute as part of its mission some considerable time before the DIT legislation was enacted. A Research Committee had been in operation under the aegis of the Academic Council since 1981, developing, promoting and monitoring research and research policies and strategies for the Institute.

Research has been a significant activity in a number of schools across the Institute, particularly in science and engineering,[3] for more than twenty-

---

3.   *Research & Development 1988–1991, A Report and Review, Dublin Institute of Technology, Kevin Street* (Dublin: City of Dublin Vocational Education Committee), 1992.

five years. In 1989 a concerted plan was adopted for its expansion and development in those areas and its extension to all other disciplines of the Institute.

Since then emphasis has been concentrated on developing research in a number of broad strategic areas, based on national priorities that corresponded to academic strengths of the Institute. These included the following areas:

- environment
- construction and property
- engineering, applied sciences and materials
- tourism and hospitality
- information technology
- biotechnology and food
- chemicals and pharmaceuticals
- applied economics, business, finance and marketing
- applied media, design, communications and social science
- music and drama.

Involving and facilitating individual members of staff in research activities has been a core strategy. There have been a number of other key activities as corollaries to this strategy – overcoming the severe problems of limited accommodation and scarcity of requisite equipment, managing each researcher's teaching timetable to facilitate her/his research work, exploiting the research activities to improve courses and generally developing and spreading an intellectually challenging research ethos across the Institute. Staff members are becoming increasingly involved in research. Postgraduate research student numbers grew from less than 150 in 1994/1995 to almost 200 in 1998/1999.

Although the Institute is not allocated specific funding in its budget for research activities, the Department of Education and Science acknowledges that under the legislation it is expected to expend some of its income for this purpose. This is in contrast with the previous situation under the aegis of the provisions of the Vocational Education Act 1930 within the City of Dublin Vocational Education Committee.

Management of research

The Postgraduate Studies and Research Committee of the Academic Council has responsibility for developing and assisting the implementation of policies in relation to postgraduate research. This committee comprises representatives of all the Faculty (Academic) Boards, the main staff grades and students.

The Postgraduate Studies and Research Committee has formed four subcommittees, each with relevant representation from across the Institute. These are:

- Postgraduate Studies Committee, the work of which is described later in this chapter
- Funding Committee, to manage the distribution of Institute research funds in the different funding schemes
- Ethics Committee, responsible for developing and administering policies relating to ethical and legal issues arising from research projects in the Institute
- Postgraduate Courses Committee, to oversee and monitor all taught postgraduate courses in the Institute.

Postgraduate Studies and Research office

The Postgraduate Studies and Research office was established in 1996 as a central resource for postgraduate research and postgraduate courses across the Institute. It has responsibility for the registration and monitoring of all postgraduate students, the general administration of the Institute's regulations for postgraduate study by research and the implementation of the quality assurance procedures in postgraduate work.

Internal funding schemes

During the past number of years the Institute has developed a number of funding schemes to encourage and facilitate staff members engaging in research, including a seed funding scheme, postgraduate scholarships, postdoctoral fellowships, a strategic research and development programme and a DIT/TCD joint research seed funding scheme.

The seed funding scheme is funded from the Institute's own resources and is aimed especially at assisting staff members to initiate research projects. Since 1986, some £200,000 has been made available in support of about fifty projects annually. In assisting over 500 projects since its inception, this scheme has played a major role in fostering a research ethos across the Institute.

The postgraduate scholarship scheme was initiated in 1994, when awards were made to twenty postgraduate students. A similar number is now awarded annually. The scheme is funded from Institute resources and is aimed at assisting staff members' research while increasing the number of postgraduate students in the Institute. Allocation of these scholarships is a two-stage process. Calls for applicant projects are made annually. Formatted applications are evaluated by the Funding Committee and the twenty qualifying applications with the highest scores are approved. The second stage consists of a call for applications for scholarships on approved projects.

A scheme to fund up to six post-doctoral fellowships (renewable for up to three years) per annum within the Institute was initiated in 1995, with the aim of further enhancing the standard of research work in key areas in the Institute. These are also funded by Institute resources.

Since 1993, the Strategic Research and Development (SRD) programme has been funded by the European Social Fund through the Department of Education and provides postgraduate students with training in research and development in strategic technological areas. The principal aims are to enhance research and development capabilities in Ireland and to strengthen links between the Institute and industry and commerce in Ireland and generally in Europe. Industry and commerce involvement is a key feature of projects under this programme. Some thirty-two postgraduate students have been recruited annually and there are currently some eighty students involved at various stages in their projects. By 1998, over seventy students had graduated with master's or PhD degrees from the programme and in general it had contributed considerably to research activity in the Institute.

The joint DIT/TCD research seed funding scheme was described in Chapter 4.

External funding

Staff members of the Institute also compete successfully for Enterprise Ireland grants for Basic and Strategic Research and for the Applied Research Programme (ARP), the Higher Education Industry Co-operation Programme, European Union (EU) Framework and other programmes, as well as grants from a range of other public bodies and private agencies. ARP grants are funded by industry and Enterprise Ireland. The industrial contribution (25 per cent of total) to these projects in the DIT in 1996 was £112,000, representing seventeen projects.

The DIT has been the recipient of substantial external research funding for some time. Since the late 1980s such research funding had been running at over £1 million per annum and in more recent years the amounts received were £2 million in 1994 to 1995, £2.6 million in 1995 to 1996 and close to £4 million in 1996 to 1997. Given the historical development of the DIT as a mainly teaching institution and the relatively restrictive nature of the legislation under which it operated prior to 1993, this has represented a substantial growth in research activity.

Funding under the HEA research scheme 1999–2001

In 1999 the DIT was awarded £8.2 million in the competitive Higher Education Authority programme for research in third-level institutions (1999–2001) for the construction of a 2,500 square metre research building to be associated with the Kevin Street college and the faculty of science. This will be the largest single investment ever in postgraduate research in the DIT. Under the project a facility for optical characterisation and spectroscopy will be developed to support activities spanning the disciplines of science, engineering and food science. It is expected to be completed in 2001.

PRODUCTIVITY OF RESEARCH IN THE INSTITUTE

Publications, both peer reviewed and others, constitute an important measure of the productivity and quality of research. Table 9.1 summarises the publications and other scholarly output of Institute staff over the period 1993–1997.

Table 9.1: Summary of the Institute's scholarly output 1993–1997						
	1993	1994	1995	1996	1997	Total
Peer reviewed publications	123	126	137	124	161	671
Other publications	56	71	80	105	148	460
Consultancies	13	12	11	17	44	97
Exhibitions	47	44	82	55	73	301
External grants	19	18	16	29	59	141

The productivity of the Institute's staff, by faculty, over the same period is shown in Table 9.2, which gives the numbers of publications, other scholarly activities and external research grants obtained.

Table 9.2: Scholarly productivity from 1993–1997 of Institute staff, by faculty			
Faculty	Peer reviewed publications	Other publications	External grants
Applied arts	96	96	16
Built environment	19	27	6
Business	69	62	5
Engineering	91	42	14
Science	260	120	59
Tourism and food	69	89	23

QUALITY ASSURANCE IN POSTGRADUATE RESEARCH WORK

In 1992, the Academic Council organized the Postgraduate Studies Committee as a subcommittee, to manage and oversee the academic quality assurance of the postgraduate research activities throughout the Institute. This committee established the first DIT register of postgraduate students in academic year 1994/1995 and drafted the quality assurance regulations and procedures for postgraduate studies by research. These regulations were submitted in draft form to the Academic Council in February 1994. After discussion within the Academic Council and throughout the Institute, and after receipt of written comments and suggestions, amendments were incorporated. The regulations were approved by the Academic Council in May 1994 and have since been widely promulgated and implemented throughout the Institute.

After two years of application, the regulations were reviewed, modified and reaffirmed by the Academic Council in May 1997.[4]

These regulations set out the terms of reference of the Postgraduate Studies Committee (now a subcommittee of the Postgraduate Studies and Research Committee of the Academic Council), the levels of postgraduate awards offered within the Institute and the range of research activities that might be approved for such postgraduate awards.

The minimum entry qualifications for each register and the application procedures are set down. The regulations describe the process of assessment of an application, the nomination of a research supervisor and advisory supervisor, where required, and the process of registration of a postgraduate student. They also set out the duties of the supervisors, the

---

4. *Regulations for Postgraduate Study by Research, (2nd ed.)* (Dublin: Dublin Institute of Technology), 1997.

relevant head of school and the postgraduate research student. Training modules in research supervision are provided for supervisors annually. Detailed procedures for the supervisor(s) and postgraduate student to agree on the proposed work, a schedule of meetings, early resolution of problems, reports on progress, application to transfer to a higher register and the submission of the thesis are set down. Furthermore, students are required to attend training modules in areas relevant to their work and present a number of seminars each year on their research.

Bi-annual progress reports are required of all registered postgraduate students and research supervisors, and are reviewed by the Postgraduate Studies Committee. Formal procedures are specified in relation to annual re-registration.

The regulations specify the format and presentation of the thesis and the three months' notice of intention required before submitting it. The examination is normally carried out by an internal examiner with research experience in an area related to the thesis topic and at least one external examiner of standing in the field of the candidate's research work. In addition to examining the master's thesis, the examiners may also test the candidate by oral examination if they consider this to be necessary. In the case of doctoral candidates, the examiners are required to organize an oral examination in which they test the candidate's knowledge of matters relevant to the thesis. Where the thesis needs to be revised and resubmitted, only one resubmission is allowed.

DEVELOPMENT CENTRES

Since 1993, the Institute has formally established a number of specialised development and consultancy centres and other units, principally to engage in desk research, development and consultancy work on contract for industry. These centres have included or now include: National Avionics Ltd., Food Product Development Centre, Industrial Control Centre, Radiation Science Centre, Tourism Research Centre, National Maintenance Centre, Timber Development Centre, Digital Media Centre, Applied Optoelectronics and Optical Communications Centre, Industrial and Engineering Optics Centre, National Logistics Centre, National Satellite Services Centre, Centre for Social and Educational Research, Building Information Centre, Irish Centre for Environmental Health, Media Production Unit and Project Development Centre.

Most of the centres have been assisted in their initial phase by state agencies such as Enterprise Ireland, drawing on EU funds, but they are encouraged to earn income as soon as possible for the services they provide.

The Institute has used rented premises, often some distance from the college sites, to accommodate most of these development centres. Consequently they have "little (if any) direct relationship with the Institute's teaching" and research within the schools.

Summary

Since the DIT was statutorily established in 1993, it has placed considerable importance on developing its postgraduate research base, producing a notable publication and research grant record over the past six years or so. At this time postgraduate research students constitute about 1.5 per cent of the full-time equivalent student population. It remains a challenge to achieve a more even spread of research throughout the schools and faculties.

The Institute also serves industry in a number of ways, including research, development and consultancy through a range of dedicated development centres. There is an important challenge to integrate this activity more closely with the core teaching and research within the schools.

Chapter 10

Accommodation and Facilities

A recurring problem throughout the history of the DIT and its predecessor colleges has been the shortage of space to accommodate the demand for student places. The colleges always attempted to serve as much as possible of the demand for places on their courses, even when this entailed a degree of overcrowding and heavy use of facilities.

The individual colleges and their satellite buildings are all located on very restricted inner city sites. The combined floor area of all the buildings owned or leased by the Institute is about 100,000 square metres, all on around four hectares of ground. Given the size of the student population, estimated to be over 12,000 equivalent full-time students, the Institute's facilities are still very deficient, despite a significant capital investment during the last fifteen years.

COLLEGE OF TECHNOLOGY, KEVIN STREET

In the immediate post World War II period, neighbouring sites extending back from Kevin Street to Camden Row were acquired in order to relieve the overcrowding in the Kevin Street college. In 1953 the Department of Education agreed to a major building programme. An extensive planning exercise was carried out to design a new building to cater for the numbers of students projected and to fulfil the educational aims of the college and its specific disciplines. In this planning process it was established, for instance, that theory classes would not be held in workshops or laboratories. Laboratories and workshops should not be used for more than 80 per cent of a nine-hour working day to allow maintenance and preparation work to be done in them. Laboratories should be designed as specialist rather than as multi-purpose laboratories. In this planning process, which included the preparation of sketches and working drawings and the specifications of furnishings, finishes, furniture and capital equipment, the senior teaching staff played a major role with the consulting engineers and architects.

The construction of the new college building was completed in 1968.

It provided about 14,000 square metres of accommodation including some 6,500 square metres of highly specialised laboratories for the engineering and science disciplines in the Kevin Street college.

An extension of close to 7,000 square metres was built during the 1980s. It opened in 1987 and provided a restaurant, library, staff office and further classroom accommodation. By 1993 the college had a total floor area of just over 22,000 square metres. During the 1990s, a site of over 0.4 hectare on Pleasants Street adjoining the college was acquired by the CDVEC to erect a research building. In spring 2000, the transfer of this property to the DIT is in progress. The funding allocated in 1999 in the Higher Education Authority programme for research in third level institutions (1999–2001) will finance the construction of a 2,500 square metres research building on this site, to be completed in 2001, to house the facility for optical characterisation and spectroscopy.

COLLEGE OF MUSIC, CHATHAM ROW AND ADELAIDE ROAD

The Adelaide Road premises were leased in the academic year 1986/1987 to supplement the Chatham Row building and cater for the music and drama disciplines. The combined floor area of the two buildings is about 2,500 square metres, one third being the leased space. Because of the special requirements of these disciplines, the facilities are very unsuitable and inadequate to cater for its small full-time student population of less than 100 and its part-time student and junior school enrolments of about 2,000. Since 1997 some speech, drama and music courses are also provided in Rathmines.

COLLEGE OF COMMERCE, RATHMINES AND AUNGIER STREET

An extension to the original Rathmines Technical Institute was built in 1944 which facilitated the enrolment of additional student numbers in the immediate post World War II period.

In 1983 Rathmines House, near the original college building, was leased to supplement the accommodation in the college.

The former Jacob's factory site on Bishop Street/Aungier Street was acquired by the CDVEC in the early 1980s for a major new building complex which would accommodate the requirements of both the College of Commerce in Rathmines and the College of Marketing and Design in Mountjoy Square. A contract to construct Phase I of this development was placed eventually in 1992 and the building was completed in 1994.

This building enabled the College of Commerce sector of the DIT to transfer from Rathmines to the new facilities in Aungier Street in the academic year 1995/1996. This new building has a floor area a little over 10,000 square metres. Phase II of this development is scheduled to begin construction in 2000 to accommodate the Marketing, and Retail and Services Management-related courses from DIT Mountjoy Square. It is envisaged that Phase II will offer an additional 15,000 square metres of floor area.

COLLEGE OF MARKETING AND DESIGN, MOUNTJOY SQUARE

In an effort to solve the accommodation problems in the school of commerce and retail distribution (then the College of Marketing and Design), which was at number 18 Parnell Square, the next door building was purchased in 1977 to accommodate the other two schools, marketing and design.

During the academic year 1983/1984 the College of Marketing and Design was transferred to temporary leased premises on Parnell Square and then in 1987/1988 to more extensive leased accommodation of about 6,500 square metres on Mountjoy Square. While this space was more extensive than that available in Parnell Square, it was not ideal in that it had been constructed as basic office accommodation. The college also relied on other satellite accommodation, also leased, to constitute a total floor area of about 9,500 square metres.

COLLEGE OF TECHNOLOGY, BOLTON STREET

The original purpose-built Bolton Street college building had about 4,500 square metres of floor area including classrooms, workshops and laboratories. Between 1926 and 1931 an extension providing an additional 1,500 square metres of workshop and classroom accommodation was added.

In the 1950s a second extension, a four storey building along King's Inn Street, was added. This provided 3,000 square metres of floor area giving additional workshop, laboratory, drawing office and classroom space.

In 1962 the Linen Hall building close to the Bolton Street college, formerly a linen mill destroyed by fire during the war of independence and rebuilt as a warehouse, was acquired by the CDVEC. The building was reconstructed and refurbished to accommodate courses in the construction trades. The School of Trades in the Linen Hall, of some 10,500 square metres floor area, was opened in 1963.

In 1981 a site which had previously been the Williams and Woods factory at the rear of the college was acquired by the CDVEC.[1] It was not until 1985 that work on a 7,900 square metres extension on this site commenced and a large part of it was first occupied in 1987. The main building on Bolton Street was considerably refurbished in 1981 and, with the extension completed in 1988, resulted in a floor area in the building of some 24,000 square metres. The original building was matched to the new extension and rendered compliant with the fire safety regulations. Student social areas were provided. New laboratories for computing, communications, advanced manufacturing and printing were installed and the administration areas refurbished. The newly extended main college, coupled with the Linen Hall building and some satellite buildings, had a floor area over 37,000 square metres.

COLLEGE OF CATERING, CATHAL BRUGHA STREET

A major element of the CDVEC's 1936 strategic plan was implemented when a new college, St Mary's College of Domestic Science, was opened on Cathal Brugha Street in 1941.[2]

A major extension to the college, providing new kitchens and larders, staff and student dining room facilities, a reception area and a student common room, was completed in January 1966.

At the time of the fifty years' celebration of the college in 1991, property had been acquired and plans begun for an extension to the college on Marlborough Street. By 1997 this extension of 3,750 square metres was opened and had increased the accommodation in the college to about 14,000 square metres. The social studies school, now part of the faculty of applied arts, was re-housed in 1995 in Rathmines House, part of the leased premises previously occupied by the College of Commerce in Rathmines.

GENERAL ISSUES ABOUT FACILITIES

The Ballymun Project proposals, with roots in the CDVEC thinking in the

---

1.   O'Dwyer, D and M O'Donnell, *A Short Historical Profile, Souvenir Booklet to Commemorate the Official Opening of the Extension to the College of Technology, Bolton Street* (Dublin: City of Dublin Vocational Education Committee), 1989
2.   O'Connor, N (ed.), *op. cit.*

1930s, emerged from the most extensive and ambitious planning process ever undertaken by the Dublin colleges. As well as orienting the colleges towards a unitary multi-level higher education institution, these proposals very clearly attempted to solve the accommodation needs definitively.

Despite the major extension to the Bolton Street college, with the acquisition of the Linen Hall premises for a School of Trades and the new college in Kevin Street, all the Dublin colleges were greatly restricted in their development during the 1970s by shortage of accommodation. Their centre-city locations offered limited scope for the expansion needed to allow more student numbers and more courses.

The constraints and limitations of accommodation and other resources continued into the 1980s. Nevertheless, this decade was a period of considerable progress for the DIT colleges as they responded to the large and relatively unsatisfied demand from both school leavers seeking full-time courses and apprentices already in employment who wished to enrol on a part-time basis. A number of options were explored, including leasing office type accommodation and industrial factory buildings adjacent to the colleges, and some such measures were taken to provide short-term solutions. Pre-fabricated buildings located close to the main buildings were also used at a number of colleges to accommodate students on a temporary basis.

The 1980s saw some enhancement of the facilities and accommodation in the DIT colleges in Kevin Street and Bolton Street, admittedly always too little and too late to match the demand.

Since the DIT was statutorily established in 1993, the pressing demand to relieve the desperate shortage of physical accommodation has continued. Some 15 per cent of its accommodation is now leased. The space per student is very low by comparison with higher education norms. DIT lacks a central library facility, a major central computing facility and any special students' buildings or student residential accommodation. The Institute has extremely limited sports facilities.

The Institute used accommodation in houses in Herbert Street and Upper Mount Street and also some rented accommodation for its industry linked development centres. In general these facilities were not very suitable for this type of activity and also, because they were scattered and some distance from the colleges, they did not generate the desirable synergy with teaching and research in the schools that might otherwise have enhanced their impact.

All of the DIT facilities were owned or leased by the CDVEC until the DIT Act was implemented on 1 January 1993, when under the provisions of this legislation, they transferred to the DIT, subject to the agreement of the CDVEC. This agreement has since been confirmed in relation to the major college buildings but the outcome still remains to be resolved in relation to some ancillary buildings and sports facilities.

In the latter context there is a 4.8 hectare sports ground in Terenure, of which the DIT continues to have a shared use. The DIT is of the view that these grounds should be transferred to it to ensure an equitable distribution of CDVEC facilities. There is also the site of over 0.4 hectare on Pleasants Street adjacent to the Kevin Street college, which was acquired to provide for a research building for the DIT and which is only being transferred to the DIT in 2000. Under the terms of the DIT Act, the Minister for Education and Science is to adjudicate on such disputed transfers.

The DIT central office has been located in rented accommodation in Upper Pembroke Street since 1993. This building currently houses over seventy staff, including those attached to the offices of the president and the secretary, the finance office, student services, admissions, academic affairs, external affairs and other central service areas. The Institute's campuses are linked together, since 1995, through an integrated telephone network with voicemail facilities as well as a computer network using leased data lines. The hub of both networks is based in the new Aungier Street building.

PHYSICAL DEVELOPMENT PLAN

In the light of the physical limitations of the current centres of the Institute, particularly in the context of its mission and aims, the Institute appointed a leading firm of architects and planners in 1995 to prepare a Physical Development Plan for the development of the Institute in its urban context until 2010.

In the preparation of this plan, the City Architect, city and traffic planners, the Eastern Health Board, Coras Iompair Éireann and the Office of Public Works were consulted. The Higher Education Authority space norms and the corresponding norms established by the University Grants Committee in Britain were used to quantify the inadequacy of the current accommodation and to provide estimates of the accommodation required in the different faculty areas. Without taking account of the need for outdoor sports accommodation, and based on the 1995 enrolments, the accommodation estimated to be required was some 90 per cent more than is currently available.

An extensive hospital site at Grangegorman in the North inner city, which had become available, was identified as providing a suitable solution to the Institute's needs over the next twenty-five years. It has a total area of over twenty-seven hectares and about half of it is currently in use as playing pitches and designated as open space in the Dublin City Development Plan. Some of the buildings could be adapted for educational purposes and would also provide suitable permanent central offices for the Institute.

The Physical Development Plan provided a detailed inventory of the present facilities including the age and floor areas of its different buildings. Overall the Institute has some 120 well equipped laboratories and eighty specialised workshops to service the diverse needs of its large student population. This range is probably wider than that available in most other Irish higher education institutions but they are mainly focussed on the undergraduate and craft and apprenticeship areas.

As part of the plan a building atlas has been prepared for all of the accommodation, as an instrument for assessing the efficiency of current usage and to assist in planning modifications for the different sites and locations.

SUMMARY

Accommodation has been limited throughout the history of the Dublin colleges. Improvements have generally been too little and have come too late to provide appreciable relief. The Physical Development Plan prepared in 1995 is designed to provide the basis for comprehensively solving the accommodation problem over the coming decade.

Chapter 11

Academic Quality Assurance in the DIT

At its formal establishment in 1970, the Academic Council was given the general functions of planning, co-ordinating and developing third level education in the CDVEC colleges. Since that time, it has contributed to the academic work of the colleges, particularly in the areas of course development and validation, examination procedures and the promotion of research. It brought about improved co-ordination of approach and stimulated discussion about developments in higher education affecting the operation of the colleges.

QUALITY ASSURANCE PROCEDURES OF THE ACADEMIC COUNCIL

In order to assist it in carrying out its work, the Academic Council established a number of subcommittees and working groups to report on specific educational and related issues and this contributed to the formulation and adoption of DIT's educational policies. These included examination regulations, appeals procedures, admissions requirements, transfer procedures, research, development and consultancy policies, reviews of DIT courses and their awards, special awards for students who demonstrated academic excellence, staff development and postgraduate studies. The work of these subcommittees and working groups assisted the Academic Council in developing procedures for the peer review of programmes and the general enhancement of academic standards in programmes leading to DIT awards.

Course evaluations

The Academic Council established Boards of Studies and Course Review Boards to satisfy itself about both the standards of proposed new courses and the operation of existing courses respectively, according to broadly specified criteria. The main objectives of these course evaluations were to:

- ensure that the standards of the courses were appropriate to the types of award proposed
- ensure that the nature and content of an approved course remained in accord with its objectives and the standards approved by the Academic Council
- confirm that an approved course kept abreast of developments in the discipline concerned
- provide constructive feedback to the Academic Council, the college and Course Committee responsible for the proposal and for developing the course, through the reports made by the evaluation Board to the Academic Council (and also, where appropriate, to the University of Dublin in respect of courses leading to its degree awards under the partnership agreement).

Between periodic course reviews, the Academic Council monitored matters affecting the conduct and standard of each course through annual reports, including examination results and external examiners' reports, submitted by the college responsible for conducting it.

These procedures were similar to those of the Council of National Academic Awards (CNAA) in Britain and also those of the National Council for Educational Awards (NCEA).

Documentation required for Boards of Studies and Course Review Boards

The documentation submitted to Boards of Studies (for initial course validation) and Course Review Boards (for periodic course review) was required to include the following:

- details about the background to the course, the need and demand for it, competing courses in Ireland and elsewhere
- resource and equipment requirements (library, computer, laboratory and other student accommodation)
- course philosophy, aims and objectives
- admission and entry standards of students, arrangements for student transfer from other courses, non-standard entrants, access courses and student numbers
- course curriculum and structure, contact hours, teaching methods, tutoring arrangements, project work and assignments, other teaching and learning measures

- course content, syllabuses, arrangements for supervised work experience, field trips, synthesis of theoretical and practical elements
- marks and standards, methods of student assessment, examination and progression requirements
- membership of course committees
- staffing details, including CVs, support staff
- facilities available and required
- professional recognition.

Memberships of Boards of Studies and Course Review Boards

Boards of Studies and Course Review Boards normally had the following membership:

- four senior academic staff of the DIT, drawn from colleges other than the one offering the programme, with special consideration given to selecting those familiar with the disciplines of the course (in the case of Course Review Boards, two of the four DIT members were drawn from the college offering the course, but from schools or departments other than that responsible for its management and day-to-day operation)
- two external nominees, one of whom was normally a senior academic in the relevant discipline in a university or other institution, with the other one usually being a leading professional practitioner in the discipline in industry or commerce.

The Board typically spent two or three days visiting the college offering the course, having received the course documentation in advance. The visitation normally included meetings with staff and students and an inspection of facilities available to students on the course. There would also normally be meetings with recent graduates in the case of existing courses. Before concluding the visit, the Board would meet in private and formulate the main points for their report. The chairperson of the Board would normally outline the main conclusions of the Board to senior staff of the college before the end of the visit. A draft report would be prepared and circulated to the Board members for consideration and approval. A favourable report would normally contain a number of observations and recommendations. An unfavourable report would require additional work by the school or department responsible for the course and further submission to the Board until the course was acceptable to it. Subsequently, the chairperson of the Board would present a report on the course to the Academic Council and at the same time forward copies of it to the college and school or department offering the course, inviting a response to Council.

External examiners

In addition to course validation and review procedures, and as another important element in the quality assurance process, the Academic Council and the DIT colleges annually appointed external examiners for each course in the Institute approved for a DIT award. The general function of external examiners, as specified in the DIT's General Examination Regulations, was to ensure that the standards achieved by students were satisfactory, as judged by their performance in examinations and/or other forms of assessment.[1] External examiners were expected to have regard to the level of award, the objectives and nature of the course and appropriate national and international standards prevailing in the discipline. They were drawn from persons of standing and experience in the relevant academic field and/or the professional practice of their discipline in Ireland or abroad. They were normally appointed for a period of three years with the possibility of an extension for one further year. External examiners were issued with the following detailed terms of reference:

• to serve as a member of the examination board for the particular (usually final) year of the course

• to assess drafts of examination papers or other material including marking and assessment schemes

• to discuss with the appropriate head of school possible changes or modifications to the draft examination papers or material, including the marking or assessment schemes

• to examine each student's marked examination scripts or other materials as considered necessary or where requested to do so by the head of school

• to monitor, where appropriate, students' course work, project work or laboratory work assessments and records or reports pertaining to such work

• to suggest where considered necessary, in consultation with the appropriate head of school and internal examiner(s), alterations to the marks awarded

• to examine students orally when this was considered necessary and appropriate

---

1.   *General Examination Regulations* (Dublin: Dublin Institute of Technology), 1990.

• to submit an annual report to the college on the examinations and standards achieved by the students.

At the end of the term of office, the external examiner was required to present a report to the college, a copy of which was also sent to the Academic Registrar for the attention of the Academic Council. This report was expected to include comments on the general standards achieved by the students and on the operation of the course, the examinations and other assessments.

DEVELOPMENTS IN QUALITY ASSURANCE AFTER THE DIT ACT 1992

The academic quality assurance procedures in the Institute emerged as a key prerequisite in relation to the Institute being given degree awarding power at the time the DIT Bill was being processed in Oireachtas Éireann. For instance, in his final response to the debate on the Bill in Seanad Éireann in July 1992, the Minister for Education, Séamus Brennan TD, said:

> The DIT will be given degree awarding powers and my target, subject to discussions, would be that within twelve months, we might be able to arrive at that position. . . It is appropriate that, before we take that final step we should have an opportunity to consult with the new Governing Body and the Academic Council as to qualitative matters. . . .

In 1993, following the statutory establishment of the DIT, the composition and functions of the Academic Council were also given a statutory basis under the DIT Act. At that time the Academic Council decided to undertake a fundamental review of its work and operating procedures and to give special attention to quality assurance as it affected all aspects of its work.

Steering committee to develop quality assurance procedures

Against this background, the Academic Council decided in March 1994 to establish a quality assurance steering committee with the then deputy president, Michael O'Donnell, as its chairperson and Thomas Duff, Joseph Hegarty and Matthew Hussey as members. The terms of reference of the steering committee were to:

- review the situation
- investigate best practices elsewhere
- produce a report highlighting the good practices already operating in the Institute
- identify issues which needed to be addressed, with special attention directed towards further enhancing quality assurance measures in the Institute.

Work of the quality assurance steering committee

The steering committee began its work by examining in detail the relevant provisions of the DIT Act and reviewing the existing quality assurance procedures in the DIT, outlined earlier in this chapter. A range of published documentation on quality assurance was studied and colleagues experienced in implementing such procedures in other university-level institutions in Ireland and abroad were consulted. The steering committee organised a one day seminar in May 1994, which was attended by some 150 staff members and was addressed by experts in the subject from Britain, the Netherlands and Ireland. Members of the steering committee made presentations outlining how its work was proceeding and invited members of the Academic Council and other staff to make submissions on any aspects considered appropriate.

Initial report of the steering committee

The steering committee prepared a first report reflecting the presentations made at the seminar and feedback received afterwards, together with their own developing views. It was submitted for consideration at a special meeting of the Academic Council in July 1994.

By then it had emerged that the main task of the subgroup was to prepare a quality assurance handbook, in the context of the requirements of the DIT legislation and the agreed desire for greater devolution of responsibilities to staff members for self-evaluation of different aspects of their work. This handbook would formally and systematically document and suitably revise the existing practices in relation to initial course approvals, on-going course reviews and procedures relating to examinations and assessments.

Quality assurance handbook

In December 1994 the steering committee tabled a draft quality assurance handbook at the Academic Council. Over the next three months the sub-group held information and consultation meetings in all of the centres of the Institute. In March 1995 the handbook was finally approved and adopted after a number of amendments had been incorporated. It was accepted as a first edition of a handbook that would be reviewed and up-dated regularly. It was also understood that in its initial implementation its guidelines would have to be interpreted in a sensitive and flexible manner. The handbook was reviewed in academic year 1996/1997 by the Academic Quality Assurance Committee of the Academic Council, in the light of the experience of its application and feedback from across the Institute. The second edition was approved by the Academic Council in May 1997 after the quality audit of 1995/96.[2]

The course quality assurance handbook set out a system of quality assurance procedures for courses throughout the Institute, as well as a system of subcommittees of the Academic Council and local Faculty (Academic) Boards and Course Committees to implement and monitor the procedures.

The subcommittees of the Academic Council, each with agreed terms of reference, were allocated responsibilities in each of the following areas: Standing, Academic Quality Assurance, Postgraduate Studies and Research, Examinations and Awards, Recruitment and Admissions, Teaching and Learning Strategy, Staff Development Strategy, Apprentice Education and Library.

As an interim measure, and until the new faculty structure is fully implemented, it was agreed that college Academic Boards (in place of the proposed Faculty Boards) be established in the six colleges.

The procedures set out in the handbook were based on the recognition of the key role that the individual staff members play in course teams and Course Committees devoted to delivering courses of the highest quality. They were also designed to devolve to the Course Committee and thence to each member of the course team the greatest degree of authority, autonomy and responsibility for the various aspects that contribute to the quality of the course(s) to which they would be assigned.

The handbook set out the procedure, with guidelines, for proposing a new course and preparing it for validation. It recommended a general format for the course document, set out the ancillary and support documenta-

---

2. *Course Quality Assurance Handbook, (2nd ed.)* (Dublin: Dublin Institute of Technology), 1997.

tion usually required, and prescribed the internal consideration of this documentation before the validation event. The handbook also outlined the formation of the validation panel and the validation process for a proposed course before it could receive final approval.

The Course Committee would prepare an annual report on its course, making a critical review of the year's operation of the course and incorporating its responses to the suggestions of the external examiners. It would make a general assessment of a number of key aspects of the operation of the course and also suggest minor modifications to the course for the following year. The annual report would be forwarded to the Faculty (Academic) Board and from there to the Academic Quality Assurance Committee of the Academic Council.

Each course would be reviewed formally at least once every five years or so. An internal self-study of the course would be the key element of this review. After the self-study was completed and a modified course document prepared, it would be considered by the Faculty (Academic) Board before examination by an external review panel. The general nature and timing of a review process were also set out for the guidance of the Course Committee.

QUALITY AUDIT 1995–1996

The DIT Act made provision that a ministerial order from the Minister for Education would give the DIT the power to make degree awards. In 1995, the Minister, Niamh Bhreathnach TD, requested the HEA to carry out an audit of the quality assurance procedures in place in the Institute. The HEA appointed an authoritative review team, the membership of which is given below, to carry out this task.

Self-evaluation the key process in the quality audit

At the start of the 1995–1996 academic year, the review team decided that its approach would be to require the Institute to carry out a "self-evaluation" and then to review the report from the Institute on this process. This approach was very similar to a quality audit in the British and various other higher education systems.

Members of the Review Team 1995–1996

Chairperson
Dr R. H. McGuigan, Provost and Pro-Vice Chancellor, University of Ulster

International academic experts
Dr Marianne Bauer, University of Gothenburg, Sweden
Christian Thune, Centre for Quality Assurance and Evaluation of Higher Education, Copenhagen, Denmark

Irish academics
Prof. John Coolahan, Education Department, St Patrick's College, Maynooth
Prof. Cecily Kelleher, Health Promotion Department, University College, Galway

Irish industrialists
Dr Tom Hardiman, Chairperson, IBM (Ireland) Ltd, Dublin
Eileen Sweeney, Senior Financial Analyst, Aer Lingus, Dublin

Secretary
Mary Kerr, Higher Education Authority

The report on the self-evaluation of the quality assessment and control procedures in the Institute was to be "concise, but comprehensive in its coverage", giving information that was "both descriptive and evaluative" and highlighting weaknesses as well as strengths. Furthermore, according to the review team, the self-evaluation was to "be placed in the context of the Institute's mission".

Detailed specification of the self-evaluation required

The review team drew up the following detailed specifications for the self-evaluation report:

- brief outline of the Institute — formal mission, aims and goals, with reference to the DIT Act and its impact on strategic planning and internal decision-making
- management and organisational structure of the Institute — organisational arrangements, oversight of academic affairs, implementation of proposed faculty structure, decision-making process and role and function of senior officers and committees, co-ordination between faculties/schools and central administration

- academic profile of the Institute — list of courses and programmes (including externally accredited courses), academic development plan, proposed new courses (undergraduate and postgraduate), together with expected year of introduction and rationale, arrangements for student transfer between courses (internally and externally), areas of research strength, strategy for development of research in the light of the DIT Act, responsiveness to local, regional, national and international needs, structure of programmes for example modularisation and semesterisation), plans for future academic structure (introduction of grade of professor, proposed nomenclature for degrees)
- quality assurance policies, structures and procedures
- course planning and design — market testing, evidence of demand or need for new programmes, curriculum design, content, innovation, organisation, procedures for internal course approval, external validation procedures, management and allocation of staff resources, assessment of relevance and effectiveness (views of students, employers of graduates, external examiners, how these are co-ordinated, follow-up action), review procedures
- strategy for teaching, learning and assessment — policies, implementation and evaluation, student progress and achievement
- quantitative data on staff and students — with comments, staff recruitment policies and procedures, terms and conditions of employment of academic staff, appraisal and advancement or reward criteria, student access and admissions procedures, equity and equality of opportunity
- staff issues — staff training and development in teaching and assessment, personnel policies in relation to management of human resources, technician and administrative support
- student issues — support systems for students, student appeals systems, involvement of students in evaluation procedures and structures
- financial position of the Institute — budget and outturn for recent years and estimated expenditure for the coming year, sources of funding, breakdown of expenditure by categories (e.g. for academic units, library and premises), financial management, autonomy, delegation and management of resources
- facilities, buildings and laboratories, in the context of student and staff numbers, location, age, details of academic support facilities — library (book stock, places per student, etc.), information and communications technology, maintenance support
- external relationships — liaison with other academic institutions, in-

dustry, commerce, public agencies, professional bodies, student and staff mobility, international links

- overall institutional self-evaluation — relative maturity of schools as regards academic development, research and other achievements
- institutional capacity for change — responsiveness to internal and external demands, needs and opportunities.

Planned review of the self-evaluation report

The review team planned to review the self-evaluation report and consider the Institute's quality assurance procedures, seeking to ensure that they were:

- consistent with the Institute's aims and objectives
- robust, rigorous and effective
- self-renewing and subject to continuous review
- able to facilitate quality improvement
- supported by students and staff
- inclusive of external involvement
- able to ensure that outcomes of the process lead to the establishment of standards which are recognised nationally and internationally and acceptable to students, employers and professional bodies.

The self-evaluation report would also assist the review team in identifying areas requiring particular attention during their visit to the Institute in March or April 1996. After that visit the team would draft its report. The Institute would have the opportunity to review and comment on the draft report of the review team. The team would submit its final report to the HEA by June 1996 and the HEA would then forward it to the Minister for Education, with comments.

Institutional self-evaluation and preparations for the visit of the review team

A quality audit office was established with a senior member of staff seconded full-time together with an administrative assistant. A dedicated steering committee of five senior staff members, including the president and the four members of the steering committee that drafted the quality assurance handbook, was also set up to expedite the process. A newsletter was issued fortnightly during the period of the self-evaluation process, to clarify the outline requirements, to inform all staff of progress and of any problems encountered and to remind them of deadlines and other matters.

In order to meet the demanding schedule for carrying out the self-evaluation and preparing a thorough self-evaluation report on the Institute as a whole, it was necessary for heads of schools to undertake self-evaluations in their schools, according to the outlines specified. It was also essential for them to place a top priority on compiling data and fulfilling other requirements for the overall report, which were communicated to them from the central office from time to time over the period of the self-evaluation.

It was also considered essential that all members of staff contribute to this process and that the maximum amount of help be recruited in order to carry it through as fully and efficiently as possible.

The president visited every school during the self-evaluation to inform staff about the process. It was a major item on the agenda of each monthly Academic Council meeting and two special meetings of the Academic Council were also held to discuss the issue. The steering committee attended a meeting of each of the Academic Boards in the main colleges and also held consultative meetings with senior administrative staff and student representatives from all the colleges.

Data and details gathered for the self-evaluation

With respect to each course in the Institute, the quality audit office compiled the composition of the Course Committee and the annual course report for the previous academic year. It also gathered the following data for each year of each course, over the previous five academic years:

- student numbers and types
- CAO/CAS first preferences (at that stage degree courses were on the CAO list and non degree courses were on the CAS list)
- spread of Leaving Certificate points of student intake
- enrolment trends
- completion rates
- teaching hours annually per student (THAS) rating for each year
- for the overall course — student contact hours and study load, senior, junior and part-time academic staff allocation, percentages achieving each grading of awards and first employment statistics for graduates.

The office also compiled brief CV details about each full-time member of staff. These included name, school, academic and professional qualifications, present staff grade, date of appointment, previous staff grade(s), nature of current appointment, specialist teaching areas, specialist research areas, teaching experience to date in the DIT, work experience before appointment, current memberships of and involvement in professional and other bodies, administrative and committee involvement in the DIT, courses and seminars attended over past three years, research involvement, publications, exhibitions or performances and any special achievements, prizes or awards.

Details about each school

The steering committee held meetings, aided by an external facilitator, with all senior staff in each school, to carry out a strengths/weaknesses/opportunities/threats (SWOT) analysis and self-evaluation of the school. These resulted in reports on each school, with the following elements: good features and strengths of the school and how they might be developed, weak features of the school and practical ways of addressing them, problems and impediments to progress and how they may be addressed practically, any relevant needs of industry or society that were not being addressed, priority actions, the impact of the DIT Act on the school, desirable developments in the school in the next ten years, new courses which should be developed in the school with priority and rationale, additional resources (staff, space, equipment, budget) required for developments over the next five years, which courses in the school were to be phased out, measures needed to improve the teaching, learning and assessment environment, the strengths and weaknesses of quality assurance procedures, the appropriate balance for the school of postgraduate, primary degree, diploma and certificate, apprenticeship and short courses in terms of staff work and student numbers, advantages, disadvantages and priority five year targets for research, development and consultancy, strengths and weaknesses of the management and organisational structure of school, measures needed to achieve improvement in the school and make it more responsive to change, ways in which the school and Institute should promote themselves in industry, business and society.

Submission of documentation for the review

After some months of drafting, extensive work in the Course Committees and Academic Boards, involvement by members of the Academic Council in workshops and submission of a large number of written submissions, the following documentation was submitted to the HEA.

1. **Volume 1 — Self-Evaluation Study**: This contained a brief outline of the DIT, the management and organisational structure of the Institute, academic profile of the Institute, quality assurance policies, structures and procedures, the financial position of the Institute, staff issues, facilities, external relationships, the Institute's capacity for change and overall institutional self-evaluation with special reference to degree awards.

2. **Volume 2 — Accompanying Documentation**: The accompanying documentation consisted of the following publications — *Quality Assurance Handbook* (1995), *Faculty Structures in Dublin Institute of Technology* (1994), *Physical Development Plan* (Scott Tallon Walker, 1996) and the Dublin Institute of Technology Act (1992).

3. **Volume 3 — Appendices**: The appendices included a historical profile of the Dublin Institute of Technology, an account of the relationship with the University of Dublin (TCD), key features of the DIT legislation, contributions made by government ministers and opposition spokespersons during the Oireachtas debates on the DIT Bill (with particular reference to the discussion on possible degree awarding powers for the DIT), apprenticeship and related craft courses, details of industrial and international links, the development of quality assurance procedures in the DIT and tables of student and staff data.

A range of supporting Institute and related documentation was also made available.

Institutional visit of the review team

In preparation for the institutional visit of the review team, copies of the Self-Evaluation Study and the Appendices were circulated for discussion in all units of the Institute. At that stage, the documents were discussed at special meetings of the Directorate, the Academic Council, each subcommittee of the Academic Council and each college Academic Board, which were attended by members of the steering committee. This committee also held meetings with student union leaders and senior administrators at that stage to review the documents. There were also meetings of staff of each school to prepare for the institutional visit.

The review team visited the Institute during the week of 29 April 1996. This visit consisted of meetings with the senior management, the steering committee, Academic Council subcommittees, staff groups, students and graduates at each site. The team also toured each site. Members of the team also attended, as observers, a number of course review events taking place during their visit.

Report of the review team

The 1996 report of the review team highlighted a number of the characteristic strengths of the Institute and outlined the progress that had been made since its formal establishment on 1 January 1993.[3]

The report noted a number of weaknesses that needed special attention, including the level of autonomy of the Institute, the high student contact hours, deficiencies in the physical plant of the Institute and the need to develop staff members with postgraduate supervision competencies.

The review team recommended "that degree awarding powers be extended to the Institute in respect of undergraduate and postgraduate courses with effect from the 1998/1999 academic year, and that the existing relationship with the University of Dublin in relation to undergraduate degrees, be phased out commencing from that date".

In its report, the review team offered a range of helpful suggestions as to how the Institute might develop. It also made a series of specific and detailed recommendations in respect of extending quality assurance arrangements to all aspects of the work and gave a high priority to developing postgraduate research. It recommended in the light of "the unique nature of the DIT as a multi-level institution" providing "an important complementary dimension to the higher education system in Ireland . . . (that) its vocational character should be preserved and nurtured and its close working relationships with both public and private sectors should be promoted further".

Ministerial order conferring degree awarding power on the Institute

The HEA endorsed the report and recommendations of the review team and forwarded them to the Minister for Education in the autumn of 1996. The resolution on the draft ministerial order, giving the power to award degrees to the Institute, was moved in Seanad Éireann in May 1997 by the Minister for Education, Niamh Bhreathnach TD. The ministerial order was signed on 15 May 1997.

---

3.   *Review of Quality Assurance Procedures in the Dublin Institute of Technology: Report of the International Review Team* (Dublin: Higher Education Authority), 1996.

BALANCE SHEET IN 1998 OF THE INSTITUTIONAL QUALITY AUDIT OF 1995–1996

The report of the review team on quality assurance procedures in the DIT was a significant academic and political watershed in the development of the Institute and was warmly welcomed by the Institute's staff. Its outcome, the authority granted to the DIT to confer its own degree awards at primary and postgraduate levels, significantly enhanced the general academic recognition and status of the Institute. The findings and recommendations of the review team helped to shape and guide the ongoing work of developing the Institute.

The review team stated that "improved prioritisation particularly in relation to academic planning" would be necessary. In relation to academic planning, the six faculty directors and four central directors were appointed and had taken up their duties at the start of academic year 1996/1997. The directors undertook an extensive consultation throughout the Institute about the new faculty structure and as a result the president submitted an amended faculty structure proposal to Governing Body in early 1997.[4] Furthermore, the Directorate initiated a process of medium to long term strategic academic and administrative planning for the Institute. The process of consultation and discussion on the Directorate's draft outline strategic plan began in 1997 in the faculties and schools. Amendments to the core plan are being proposed and a "bottom-up" contribution to the strategic plan is being developed.

The review team suggested the expansion of student representation on the Academic Council and its subcommittees "in order to secure an appropriate level of student feedback". The Institute acted on this suggestion and extended to three the number of student representatives on all of these bodies as well as on Faculty (Academic) Boards, and one student for each year of the course on Course Committees.

The review team was of the opinion that "insufficient emphasis is given to the promotion of self-learning by the student" and that the Institute should "review its course curricula, course organisation, length of academic year and the teaching and commitments of staff and use its management discretion to deploy staff resources in such a way as to encourage and promote the expansion and development of research and scholarly work". This was fully accepted by the Institute, which began the process

---

4. *Faculty, School and Departmental Structures for the Dublin Institute of Technology* (Dublin: Dublin Institute of Technology), 1997.

of planning the requisite changes in teaching methods. This was done particularly through the Teaching and Learning Strategy Committee of the Academic Council, by discussing the implications throughout the Institute, by systematically developing the IT networking of the Institute to facilitate new approaches to teaching and learning and by increasing the staff development budget to allow staff time and resources to become involved in these developments. This work is continuing.

In relation to the "phased approach to the development of postgraduate teaching and research work which is now being implemented by the Institute", experienced advisory or mentoring supervisors have been appointed with all inexperienced supervisors to facilitate the induction and training of research supervisors. Furthermore, a series of training modules on issues relating to research supervision (regulations for postgraduate study by research, project planning, assessment of progress, report writing, thesis writing and thesis submission), are now run each year for research supervisors by the Postgraduate Studies and Research office. After extensive consultation, the second edition of the Institute's Regulations for Postgraduate Studies by Research was approved by the Academic Council in April 1997 and distributed to all academic staff in the Institute. A central postgraduate studies and research office has been organised since 1996 to provide day to day advice and guidance to both supervisors and postgraduate students.

The review team suggested that "human resource policies and contract terms should be reviewed by the Institute in the context of promoting both research and innovation in teaching and learning". Under the provisions of the DIT Act, the Institute has only limited freedom and flexibility in relation to staff contracts. Contract terms for academic staff members are currently the subject of national negotiations, in which the Institute is a minority party. Nevertheless, it is anticipated that the work outlined above, to reduce the students' class contact time, will contribute considerable flexibility in staff time tabling to facilitate research and teaching and learning innovation. Increased investment in staff development has also contributed to this development. An annual competitive scheme of bursaries for research and development projects in areas of teaching and learning innovation was introduced in 1997 for staff across the Institute.

The review team noted correctly that the "implementation of quality improvement in course content and delivery" had "been constrained, for example, in relation to involving students in the evaluation of their courses and their general educational experience", in spite of the "paramount need for student involvement in any quality assurance process". The Institute acted on this recommendation in the review of the Institute's quality assurance procedures. This review produced the second edition of the Course Quality Assurance Handbook (approved by the Academic Council in April 1997) and involved extensive staff and student input during academic year 1996/1997. Additionally courses hold at least one staff/student meeting during the academic year through which many improvements in the course administration are carried out. It is also fully realised that student consultation and feedback will also be of key importance in the efforts to reduce student class contact time and develop more student/learner centred approaches to the work of the Institute. The implementation of students' feedback on their courses continues to be an industrial relations issue on a national scale.

As recommended by the report, the "induction of new students requires careful attention and the communication to them of all relevant course materials and data is of importance to their successful recruitment." Each September, major induction events are organised for new students in each DIT site. Each student is supplied with a general student handbook. A specific course book, together with a tour of the facilities and talks on a range of academic, social and recreational aspects of Institute life, are presented to the different class groups. In each college a team, including academic, counselling and chaplaincy staff, organises these events. The Institute is developing a Student Charter, a draft of which is under discussion with student representatives.

"The physical plant and facilities of the Institute vary in quality from site to site. Some locations enjoy modern buildings and excellent infrastructure while others must be regarded as inappropriate and less than adequate for a third level educational institution." The facts behind this accurate evaluation by the review team have occupied the attention of the Directorate for some years and are slowly being remedied as funds become available. In relation to physical planning the Institute has long laboured under the limitations imposed by its restricted accommodation and available site areas. Therefore, it attaches high priority to progressing its Physical Development Plan. Such progress will be vital if the Institute is to respond to such critical aspects as providing adequate office accommodation for staff, library, social and recreational facilities for students and laboratory and workshop space to support its research development plans.

The new extension to DIT at Cathal Brugha Street, completed in 1997, has helped to improve the provision in that area. A number of neighbouring houses have been purchased near both Kevin Street and Bolton Street colleges, which will provide improvements in accommodation for staff on those sites at an early stage. Construction of the extension (Phase II) to DIT at Aungier Street is to commence in 2000. Discussions to progress the development of the major site at Grangegorman, as indicated in the Physical Development Plan, are also being pursued.

Possible application of the universities legislation to the Institute

With regard to the comment of the review team in relation to extending features of the universities legislation to the DIT, the Institute sought designation as a university within the Universities Bill as it was being processed through the Oireachtas. However, the Minister for Education decided that the Section 9 process of the Universities Act should assess the Institute's application. The assessment of the Institute under this process was outlined in Chapter 6.

Summary

The development and growth of higher education in Ireland in the 1970s led to increased government involvement as well as increased uncertainty and disquiet within the higher education institutions. In the Dublin colleges, the Academic Council was formally established in 1970 to oversee its higher education programmes. It served to improve the integration of the colleges, raise the level of the academic activities and introduce quality assurance procedures.

After the DIT was statutorily established in 1993, the Academic Council was re-organised and a more formalised approach to quality assurance procedures was developed, systematised and implemented for undergraduate and postgraduate courses and postgraduate research work. The enhancement of the quality assurance procedures represented an institutional commitment to the continuing improvement of standards and was based on devolving considerable autonomy to Course Committees and individual teaching staff members.

The institutional quality audit in academic year 1995/1996 led to the achievement of degree awarding power up to the highest postgraduate level for the Institute from September 1998. This was a major new level of academic recognition for the DIT.

The processes of preparing for the audit and the audit itself were processes of high intellectual achievement within the Institute. The preparation process was a new experience that engaged members of the Institute in widely participatory and constructive self-evaluation exercises at all levels and in all schools. The audit was a deep-going evaluation of the Institute, its quality assurance procedures and educational ethos, by a prestigious international team of academic and industrial experts. It largely confirmed the internal view of the quality and robustness of the Institute's systems and this was a major boost to morale throughout the Institute.

Furthermore, the review team made a number of constructive recommendations and pointed to strategic paths that the Institute should take to make progress — weaknesses to remedy and strengths to be improved upon — many of which are still to be fully implemented. The provisions of the Qualifications (Education and Training) Act 1999, which includes arrangements for quality assurance within the higher education sector, will also have considerable implications for the DIT.

A View of the Future of the DIT

Chapter 12

The Challenges Facing the DIT Beyond 2000

The outcome of the Section 9 process of the Universities Act 1997, through which the DIT sought to be designated as a university, was a rebuff to the Institute. It postponed reconsideration of the issue for at least three to five years. At the same time the Qualifications (Education and Training) Act 1999 called for a redefinition of the Section 9 process such as to lead to a type of university that would not be designated under the Universities Act but under this new Act. Essentially this would be a university of technology or technological university. Therefore such a designation is likely to become the objective of the Institute in the immediate years ahead.

Many of the developmental aims of the Institute were outlined in the various submissions to the review team, which undertook the audit of quality assurance procedures in 1995/96, and the review group, which evaluated the Institute for designation as a university under the Universities Act in 1997/1998. These aims need to be developed further in a systematic fashion. The observations and recommendations in the reports of both of these evaluations provide strategic guidelines for the Institute over the next five to ten years.[1] These also need to be debated, clarified and adopted as policy.

In particular the multi-level nature of the Institute needs to be defined and declared. The implications need to be fully articulated in terms of priorities, funding, physical resources and staff allocations, as well as staff recruitment and promotion. The complementary aspects of the different levels must be developed and exploited. In this regard the dangers of academic drift must be fully considered in the planning process.

---

1. *Review of Quality Assurance Procedures in the Dublin Institute of Technology: Report of the International Review Team, op. cit.*; *Review of the Application by the Dublin Institute of Technology for Establishment as a University under Section 9 of the Universities Act (1997): Report of the International Review Group to the Higher Education Authority* (Dublin: Higher Education Authority), 1998; *Recommendations of the Higher Education Authority to Government in Accordance with the Terms of Section 9 of the Universities Act 1997, Concerning the Application by DIT for Establishment as a University, op. cit.*

Internal as well as external influences will shape the actual development of the Institute over the coming period. The external factors will include government and European Union (EU) policies, technological and economic change, and societal developments. The internal factors will include the Institute's own vision for the future — the path it chooses to travel, the unity of purpose of its members and the flexibility and relevance of its responses to external challenges. The success of the DIT will depend on its collective ability to understand the external factors and manage its forces and resources to respond effectively to the opportunities and challenges. A further, not inconsiderable, prerequisite is the establishment of measurable parameters of success in different activities.

The strategic plan must clarify what the Institute intends to do with the available resources in the arenas open to it and within the evolving political, social, economic and physical constraints. Such a strategic plan must build on the present situation, and take account of the dynamics of each of the key external and internal factors, which must be carefully studied and evaluated. The plan must be inspired by a realistic and challenging vision of what the Institute plans to achieve. It is essential that a broad consensus be developed regarding the evaluation of the current state of development of the Institute, the understanding of the key factors affecting its further development and the vision of its future. Out of such a broad philosophical consensus across the Institute community, a viable plan of action to which most members would subscribe, can logically emerge.

PLANNING FOR THE FUTURE

Development of a strategic plan to 2005

Strategic planning involves a widespread consultative and participative process in an institution, designed to map out in some detail its development path for the next five years or so. Within the DIT it requires:

- to be founded on an understanding of the culture of the Institute
- an inspirational expression of the academic, quality improvement and other organisational targets over the period of the plan based on promoting professional growth of staff
- a thorough reflective self-evaluation of the functioning of the Institute and its faculties, schools and other sections, over the past number of years and an action plan for the future
- a clear statement of how the constraints of funding, accommodation, government policies, demography, local, national and international fac-

tors, social, economic and technological contexts, organisational inertia and internal impediments to change and improvement in the Institute will be overcome.

The strategic plan must be sufficiently flexible to engage every development and activity over the next five years and more. Major events that cannot be anticipated, and that can have significant impact on the plan, will inevitably happen. Therefore the strategic plan will be at best a rolling plan that must be monitored, changed, corrected and improved as events unfold and experience develops. The DIT must develop contingency plans for such eventualities, not merely react to them as they arise.

The DIT, an institution of higher education largely dependent on public funding and subject to public regulation, must develop and maintain effective relationships with the Department of Education and Science and other public bodies and representatives. These need particular attention in the process of strategic planning.

Constructing the plan

Such a thorough-going process, embracing every section of the Institute — staff and students — requires the participation of the widest cross-section of the staff at all levels. It is therefore a process that must be founded on teamwork among all members of the Institute. Such a foundation will also give the greatest assurance that the plan will be viable. It requires organisation and leadership in order to give it focus and ensure an overall integrated and institutional structure in the eventual strategic plan. The leadership must help to guide the difficult process of setting and agreeing the various priorities and of balancing between short-term and medium-term perspectives across the Institute.

Mechanisms for implementing strategies

In a large educational institution such as the DIT a strategic plan may not call for major change in all activities. It is likely that a substantial range of activities would be continued with relatively slight modifications. But whether proposed changes are major or minor, they need careful planning, inspiration and commitment.

A vital aspect of the implementation of a strategic plan is change and improvement. Change tends to emerge from some deficiency in or dissatisfaction with aspects of the current situation, and can give rise to disquiet amongst staff. This has indeed been apparent in the DIT over the past number of years, where the change underway and a degree of uncertainty about the future have given rise to discontent in many areas. Implementing change requires that all staff participate in the development and have a significant role to play in the process. Clarity, openness and trust are needed. Effective leadership involves empowering staff members at all levels so that they have ownership of the changes and improvements envisaged.[2] In this respect, as in the overall elaboration of a strategic plan, extensive consultation, communication and assurance are vital.

Communication

In the process of developing the strategic plan and subsequently implementing it, effective communication between the different sections of the Institute will be of key importance. This will mean representative meetings, consultation meetings, general staff meetings, seminars and workshops, together with an Institute newsletter, bulletins and written feedback. In particular the main decisions and activities of the Governing Body, Academic Council, Directorate and each Faculty (Academic) Board, together with other matters of academic and other interest, should be made available to staff on the Institute's intranet and in all branch libraries throughout the Institute.

Furthermore the annual and other reports of each section of the Institute (Governing Body, Academic Council, Academic Council Subcommittees, Faculty (Academic) Boards, schools, departments, course committees, library, student services, personnel, computer centre, etc.) should be made readily available.

Of course a key requirement in communication is absorbing the message, even — indeed especially — when it is unpleasant and/or critical. Another requirement that is often difficult is the need to form and hold as critically objective a view of the current situation and its dynamic as possible, and to distinguish between what might be the optimistically desirable and the actual reality. A genuinely participative, partnership approach will help to ensure such communication is effective.

Monitoring the implementation of the plan

It is primarily the responsibility of the president and Directorate to lead, oversee and facilitate the implementation of the strategic plan, working

---

2.   Kouzes, J M and Posner, B Z, *The Leadership Challenge* (San Francisco: Jolley-
     Bass Publishers), 1995.

through the faculty and other structures of the Institute. However, a well established partnership across the Institute would strongly underpin this task. Each DIT Annual Report should include a review of the implementation of the strategic academic and physical policies as well as a summary of the developments in these policies over the period. In carrying out this responsibility the directorate should prepare an annual review and progress report, together with an academic action plan for the following year, with tactical priorities based on the overall strategy.

EXTERNAL FACTORS

Government policy

The increasing involvement of the government in higher education over the past thirty years, and some of the changes that have followed, have been outlined in Chapter 3.

In 1995, the government's White Paper on education set out the framework for the development of higher education in Ireland in the years ahead and outlined the policies of the government for the sector.[3] The Institute should pledge its commitment to playing its part in implementing these policies, responding effectively and efficiently to the challenges of "the projected growth of numbers participating in higher education". Policies arising from this and the commitment of the Institute to the concept of wider access to third level education should find expression in the strategic plan.

The government has set out other strategies for the education and training of the unemployed and other socially disadvantaged members of the community.[4] The Institute's policy is to collaborate with the Department of Education and Science and other agencies in these policies of inclusion, and DIT must seek necessary resources to fully participate in determining the best ways of progressing this socially desirable programme.

The demographic trends and related suggestions made in reports of agencies such as the Higher Education Authority (HEA), must also be considered and incorporated in any strategic planning.[5]

The aims of Irish industrial and general economic development policy,

3. *Charting our Education Future, op. cit.*
4. *Operational Programme for Human Resource Development 1994–1999* (Baile Átha Cliath: Oifig an tSoláthair), 1994.
5. *Report of the Steering Committee on the Future Development of Higher Education* (Dublin: Higher Education Authority), 1995.

as articulated by the government and its agencies such as Enterprise Ireland, include the encouragement of local small and medium enterprises as well as attracting substantial high technology investment from abroad.[6] On the world stage there is increasing industrial and economic competition. It is the policy of the DIT to continue to play a major role in helping the economic development process by providing advanced and flexible education, research and training opportunities that will help to keep Ireland at the forefront of technical advance and industrial development in this new industrial revolution.

The technology foresight exercise undertaken in 1998/1999 by the Irish Council for Science, Technology and Innovation on behalf of the Minister for Science, Technology and Commerce set out a range of research and development priorities for Ireland.[7] These key areas include:

• chemicals and pharmaceuticals
• information and communications technologies
• materials and manufacturing processes
• health and life sciences
• natural resources (agriculture and food, marine, forestry)
• energy, transport and logistics
• construction and infrastructure.

All of these areas are disciplines that have been developed within the Institute over a long time by DIT staff so that there is a considerable body of experience, learning, expertise and publications in these fields within the Institute. The recommendations in the technology foresight reports present particularly graphic and clear signposts and opportunities for the development of the Institute and its activities, both in research and taught courses at all levels.

National and international context

Within the country, which has long had a deep love of learning and respect for education, there is growing recognition of the importance of educational attainments. Higher education remains strongly correlated with

---

6. *Shaping Our Future – A Strategy for Enterprise in Ireland in the 21st Century* (Baile Átha Cliath: Oifig an tSoláthair), 1995; *Ireland, National Development Plan, 2000–2006* (Baile Átha Cliath: Oifig and tSoláthair), 1999.
7. *Technology Foresight Ireland – an ICSTI Overview* (Dublin: Forfás), 1999.

economic and career success.[8] In the next decade and beyond, young people who are now students will graduate to become leaders in industry, commerce and society. It is part of the Institute's mission to offer courses and programmes, in a stimulating environment and an ethos of learning and scholarship, where the most advanced information and communications technologies are integrated with these programmes. During students' time in the Institute, there must be a committment to providing them with an education appropriate for a rounded intellectual and personal formation, helping to develop in them an eagerness to learn and a capacity for intellectual growth throughout life. This education will equip students with the learning capabilities to acquire the knowledge necessary for them to function well in their chosen careers in a rapidly changing technological world. It will enable them to provide leadership naturally and confidently in Irish and European society in the new century.

The extension of the European Union (EU) towards Eastern Europe, and the related diminution of subventions to Ireland, will present challenges and opportunities. It is possible that greater numbers of students from the continent may wish to study for at least part of their courses in the Institute. The provision of English language teaching to large numbers of such students and their effective integration into courses in the Institute will be a challenge, but will open the opportunity of using distance teaching and learning techniques before they travel to Dublin. Strong collaborative links with institutions across the continent will be needed for this. Opportunities to participate in helping to modernise institutions in Eastern Europe, particularly in regard to advanced technologies, will also emerge in the years ahead.

Technological developments

It is recognised that this is an era of rapid social and economic change, greatly influenced by information and communication technology and other leading edge technologies. The Bangemann Report, for instance, acknowledged that "throughout the world, information and communication technologies are generating a new industrial revolution already as significant and far-reaching as those of the past. It is a revolution based on information, itself the expression of human knowledge."[9]

The changes in computer and telecommunications technologies have the potential to fundamentally change the way the DIT functions and

---

8. *Human Resource Development* (Baile Átha Cliath: Oifig an tSoláthair), 1997.
9. *EU, Europe and the Global Information Society* (Brussels: European Union), 1995.

teaches. They change disciplines and suggest new disciplines. The Institute must clear the way in its strategic plan for the acceptance and constructive development of these changes, and seek to be in the forefront of these developments. For instance, the Institute should play a leadership role in developing the training, techniques and all other aspects of electronic commerce (e-commerce) and, indeed, electronic teaching through telematics and distance teaching and learning techniques, and other electronic social, cultural and personal activities.

Demographic changes

Many different aspects of the population of Ireland are in rapid change, such as its geographic spread, its social, professional and employment profile, and its age profile. Consequently the educational services that will be required in five to ten years' time will be different from those needed today. The Institute's strategic plan must reflect this reality.

The broad changes in the age profile of the population were indicated in a Forfás report in 1996. The percentage of the population in the 0–14 ear old age group fell from 31 per cent in 1981 to 27 per cent in 1991, and is projected to fall to 22 per cent in 2001 and 17 per cent in 2011. Even though the numbers of students at second level continued to increase in the 1980s and to the mid-1990s, they are projected to fall steadily from 1998 to 2010. The number in the Leaving Certificate cohort in 1998 was about 66,000 and an HEA study of 1995 projected the numbers in this cohort each year would steadily fall over the decade from 2000 to 2009. While the fraction of that cohort entering higher education was projected to continue to rise from about 45 per cent in 1999 to over 50 per cent in 2010, late entry students, students from abroad and mature students were expected to hold the total entry numbers to higher education at about 35,000 over that decade. Projections so far into the future must be considered in the light of the assumptions underlying them, but there seems little doubt but that the competition for students will sharpen considerably and this must shape aspects of the strategic plan of the Institute.

Competition in higher education

The competition in higher education takes a number of different forms. There is the competition of example, fuelled by the contrast in facilities and resources between the different institutions. This plays a major role in the competition for students at undergraduate and postgraduate levels. There is competition for funds from government, EU and private sources.

There is competition for technical and other discipline niches in the academic marketplace. There is competition for highly qualified staff.

Each higher education institution in Ireland faces this competition and, generally based on its strengths, sets priorities to develop and make progress. In its strategic plan, the DIT must not only form a realistic depiction of the place of the Institute in the educational scene, but also review and evaluate the position of the other major institutions as well. The DIT must also face the issue of competition from international institutions already making inroads by means of distance teaching and even establishing campuses in Ireland. This will condition part of its strategy.

Qualifications (Education and Training) Act 1999 and National Qualifications Framework

The Qualifications (Education and Training) Act 1999 was a significant piece of legislation, which, along the lines of the 1995 White Paper on education, will affect the forward progress of the DIT in the next decade and beyond. The Act proposed the establishment of a National Qualifications Authority. In turn, this Authority will establish and maintain a national qualifications framework, supported by quality assurance procedures, in which the DIT will play a key part. The specific role of the Institute and how this may guide its activities has yet to be elaborated. But it would appear that some provisions of the new Act significantly amend the DIT Act.

Regardless of the outcome of any further Section 9 process for the DIT, the Institute will remain under the aegis of this Act. Familiarity with the terms of this Act and constructive involvement in the national qualifications framework will be key elements of the DIT's strategic plan.

INTERNAL FACTORS

Vision and leadership

In elaborating the vision, the collective mind of the Institute must rise above the routine continuation of what is there now to arrive at proposals that can be inspirational and forward focussed. It is safe to say that there can be little chance of implementing a so-called strategic plan unless it is inspired by and suffused with a clear vision of the future. This vision must evolve from the membership of the Institute and be drawn together by the leadership. It should be a major determinant of the broad unity of purpose within the Institute's community. The vision for the Institute must consist of broadly attainable goals that are challenging to all staff, but which will be felt internally and perceived externally to be of significance.

Included in the vision should be a statement of ethical values and educational philosophy to underpin the work of the Institute. In the context of the changing nature of knowledge and the need to prepare students for life and work, education requires a greater emphasis on vocational instruction in this philosophy than before. It should also include consideration of the potential for social divisiveness in the binary system in higher education and how the Institute will seek to avoid the danger of such divisiveness. It should contribute to the democratic vision and general welfare of society. In this sense it should re-emphasise the primary commitment of the Institute to the students, to supplying the country with women and men trained in the higher level knowledge and skills needed for the civilization of the 21st century, intellectually, socially and culturally mature, devoted to critically pursuing the truth and capable of being productive citizens of Ireland and Europe.

Organisation

The Institute is currently engaged in an academic reorganisation to a discipline based faculty structure, with related schools grouped together in each faculty. The Governing Body reaffirmed this new structure, originally rooted in the Ballymun Project proposals of 1969 and proposed in the IPA study of 1993, in 1995 and again in 1997. Each faculty will be under the academic leadership of a Faculty Board, chaired by the relevant faculty director, with a range of responsibilities as set out in the Course Quality Assurance Handbook.[10] An important task of the next two or three academic years will be the development of cohesion and unity of purpose in the six faculties and their Faculty Boards. This task will be the particular responsibility of the faculty directors.

But while cohesion is to be a key early goal in each faculty, this should not be an inwardly looking cohesion that might exclude essential cross-faculty collaborative programmes. It is a statutory responsibility of the Academic Council to ensure the development of effective collaboration between faculties in the design and development of courses and programmes with cross-discipline aspects.

A most appropriate way to legislate the governance of the Institute would be through the development of a charter. The Universities Act en-

---

10. *Course Quality Assurance Handbook (2nd ed.), op. cit.*

visaged a charter for each university and the Qualifications (Education and Training) Act envisaged one for each regional Institute of Technology. Some progress was made during 1996/1997 in drafting a DIT charter which would serve essentially as the constitution of the Institute. But to give it life, it needs to be brought forward to all members of the DIT and developed in the spirit of partnership. The various internal statutes and regulations will be developed and adapted from current regulations to be compatible with the charter.

Academic development — general principles

The character of the DIT as an integrated multi-level higher education institution offering a range of courses from apprenticeship to master's degrees, together with a range of postgraduate research activities meriting awards from postgraduate diploma to doctoral level, must be clearly articulated and developed. The relative proportions of the activities and resources of the Institute devoted to each level of educational provision may change with the evolving situation and market forces, but the same fundamental range and blend of elements will remain.

The Institute offers a framework of educational opportunities, with transfer possibilities and ladders at all appropriate stages, encompassing full-time, part-time, block release and other flexible access modes. In this context the DIT has much to offer the proposed new national qualifications framework. The Institute will continue to explore ways of improving the flexibility, accessibility and user-friendliness of the Institute to all sections of the society with which it interacts, and especially to those who are employed in industry or commerce and wish to improve their academic qualifications, as well as to those who are unemployed and are experiencing difficulty in obtaining access to third level education, and those who seek a second chance of higher education later in life than usual.

The academic activities of the Institute are designed and monitored in accordance with the general quality assurance regulations drawn up by the Academic Council. In codifying the range of its monitoring and reporting arrangements, and specifying lines of responsibility, these regulations seek to guide each course and optimally match its standard and delivery to the needs of the student, industry and society. They seek also to imbue those involved in the delivery of a course, including staff and students, with an ethos of continuing improvement in all aspects of teaching and learning, training and personal formation. These regulations and procedures themselves are also regularly reviewed and improved in the light of experience.

Teaching and learning are complex and rapidly changing processes, especially in this era of mass higher education. There is an intellectual and emotional interaction between the teacher with her/his skills, knowledge, character and motivation, and the students with their range of talents and levels of participation. The teaching and learning facilities and environment play an important role in these processes.

The policy of the Institute must be to achieve and reward excellence in teaching at all levels. It must also ensure that assessment of student performance is closely matched to course aims and students' needs. This necessitates the recruitment of teaching staff of the highest quality, followed by proper induction to help and inspire them to develop and maintain a high level of motivation. It also entails the recognition and encouragement of their efforts as they engage in effective teaching. It requires the provision of the full range of advanced facilities and techniques — to allow the delivery of an appropriate blend of lectures, practicals, tutorials, computer-assisted learning, multimedia methods, self-paced learning and distance teaching — to achieve the academic goal.

A fundamental facility to underpin and facilitate the new and emerging integrated educational process required will be the Institute library system. The Institute has plans to develop its library facilities including the branch libraries in the separate centres, increasing the student reading space, developing the book and journal holdings, while continuing to enhance their computerisation and accessibility and upgrading to a state-of-the-art library using computer networks and other electronic and multimedia technologies. This will involve the reorientation and retraining of teaching staff in relation to the nature of courses and teaching techniques to more fully exploit the educational riches that are available in the library and accessible through various electronic databases and networks.

In order to achieve and maintain the excellence in teaching and learning to which the Institute is pledged, the Academic Council has established a committee on Teaching and Learning Strategy and a Teaching and Learning Resource Centre. This centre will enable the staff of the Institute to study and assess third level teaching practices and innovative assessment methods, as well as promote better student learning strategies in all areas of its activities. It will focus also on the development and exploitation of the new library and IT facilities. It will commission and conduct research into and devise experimental programmes applying new thinking to teaching, learning and assessment processes. It will advise and train the academic and other staff within the Institute on its findings on these matters. The aim of the centre will be to become a powerhouse for advancement of the higher education process in Ireland and internationally.

A clear policy of continuing to improve the Institute, founded on partnership across the staff grades and across the disciplines, must be coupled with the appropriate devolution of authority, ownership and management decision-making in respect of each course and programme, to the faculties, schools, course committees and to lecturers and students involved in its education and training processes. In the policies and procedures outlined in the Course Quality Assurance Handbook, the course committee is given the front-line responsibility for managing the design and delivery of its course.

Programmes at each level need to be developed and nurtured. The excellence and coherence of each course, together with the value of the award and the dignity and contribution of the staff involved, need to be copperfastened and reaffirmed. But the courses need to be considered also in the light of the new national qualifications framework and designed or redesigned for optimum transferability of credits within the Institute and externally in Ireland and internationally.

In order to improve the flexibility and accessibility of the courses and programmes offered in the Institute, it is desirable that courses be progressively modularised, with each module assigned a credit weighting of the appropriate level in the European Credit Transfer System (ECTS). When a module is passed, the student will be accorded academic credits and will accumulate these to qualify for a certificate, diploma or degree award, as appropriate. This will facilitate students seeking to pursue courses on a full-time, part-time or other flexible access mode, including distance education and summer and other vacation modules and courses.

All of these quality assurance processes and the Institute's experience of implementing them can be related to the national qualifications framework and related systems. The DIT's experience with quality assurance procedures can contribute to the shaping of these systems.

The Institute has long established links with Irish industry and commerce, professional bodies, government and other agencies at individual, research/development and institutional levels. These help the Institute to identify the needs of industry and society and enable it to respond quickly and flexibly to them. It is the policy of the Institute to extend, enhance and formally structure these links in order to respond more effectively to the education and training needs of Irish society. In the design of and justification for each new programme of the Institute, the Course Quality Assurance Handbook prescribes, as fundamental criteria, the examination of the market for the programme and the needs for it in industry and society in general.

It is an established priority of the Institute that research activities be enhanced in all its schools. These activities assist in improving the quality of the syllabus content, teaching and learning. The Institute has adopted the policy of encouraging research by reducing impediments for existing staff to participate as well as facilitating the employment of additional full-time researchers, or part-time industry based researchers. The Institute is committed to increasing the number of postgraduate research students in each faculty and in each school, so that the overall postgraduate student enrolment will constitute 10 per cent by about 2010.

Research and consultancy activities allow the staff of the Institute to make their extensive range of expertise available to industry and commerce. Research work in the Institute will continue to have mainly an applied, technological emphasis, with a focus on the needs of industry or commerce and society. This emphasis and character will continue to be a hallmark of most of the DIT's work. In this context the Institute is developing policies on intellectual property rights and technology transfer which will enable and enhance the closer involvement of the staff of the Institute with industry and commerce.

The Institute has for many years provided a wide range of industry and commerce led programmes of continuing education as well as short courses in different discipline areas, responding to specific training needs. The Institute is undertaking a fundamental reappraisal of its current provision in this area to ensure that it provides students in the new century with an education that will equip them with the knowledge and skills sufficient to engage the challenges of industry and commerce. It must meet the demands from potential participants to enhance their expertise and update their skills and competencies. A continuing education unit will be established to promote and co-ordinate this important aspect of the Institute's mission. The general policy of the Institute in relation to such courses is to assign academic credits at appropriate levels to them, as it is doing with its other programmes, so that the participants can accumulate academic credits towards certificate, diploma or degree awards. These courses will also be appropriately monitored by the Institute's quality assurance procedures.

Physical resources

There is a fundamental link between the provision of the highest standard of general facilities — classrooms, laboratories, equipment, libraries, telecommunications — and the assurance of academic quality. The Institute must make budgetary provision to maintain its facilities at the highest standard for the benefit of the whole academic community. The fact is that the facilities and accommodation in the most recently built section are a benchmark for all other areas. Accommodation in the older buildings now suffers seriously on this comparison. This means that a priority must be given to the refurbishment and/or the replacement of older buildings.

Appropriate accommodation and facilities must be made available for all planned activities, and all accommodation maintained in the safest and most professional manner with suitable technologies to underpin the full institutional commitment to the highest quality environment.

In committing to develop the buildings, land and resources to optimally achieve the teaching/learning aims of the Institute, the strategic plan should also consider how it might optimise the use of buildings and facilities in a cost-effective way, including at times when they are vacant.

There is a pressing need for a doubling of the Institute's physical resources for academic, social, sporting and cultural purposes, as outlined in the Physical Development Plan. The Grangegorman proposal should be progressed quickly in the coming five years. The strategic plan will offer the perspective of solving the accommodation problems as early as possible over the next decade.

Financial autonomy

Probably the single greatest limitation on the ability of the Institute to set and implement priorities is its virtually total reliance on exchequer funding, mainly from the Department of Education and Science. The funding arrangements and lines of responsibility set out in the DIT Act are adequate for the majority of the relatively routine base-load activities of the Institute. But they place strict limitations on the autonomy and freedom of action of the Institute's management to optimally and flexibly recruit, reward and deploy its staff, to sell, buy or rent accommodation as required and to acquire other specialised resources.

Thus far the Institute has not managed to develop substantial income independent of the direct government subvention. However, it is of the greatest importance that such sources be developed in the years immediately ahead in order to create the autonomy so urgently needed.

For the DIT to be in a position to enhance the academic freedom of the Institute and to allow greater flexibility in its development, it probably needs to raise some 10 per cent of its revenues from sources other than the exchequer in the next five years or so. Consequently the Institute needs to put in place procedures, structures and staffing to raise funds through a range of activities.

Among the activities which might be planned to generate income are the following:

- research and consultancy
- advisory think tanks for industry, state and EU agencies
- campus companies
- campus services
- short industry-led courses
- international (non-EU) students
- donations for specific projects
- industrial collaboration on specific projects
- local government collaboration on specific projects
- collaboration with other organisations, sporting, social, etc.
- an international foundation with charity status
- bequests and others.

Management information system

This Information Technology (IT) age has deep implications for all aspects of education and training. The DIT aims to be in the forefront of the evaluation, use and development of IT for internal and external applications. It aims to incorporate the latest pedagogic applications of IT into all disciplines and courses throughout the Institute, as appropriate. It also aims to provide courses in, and research into, IT at all levels and in all disciplines. A new network-based management information system for the Institute will be introduced on a phased basis from 2000. This will make a wide and developing range of student, course and school management information readily available throughout the Institute. All individual staff members will have networked PCs with email and internet facilities. This plan will require a commitment to a robust and fully supported physical infrastructure and software provision. It must be extended to all appropriate areas in the Institute, and it must be continually and critically developed and grown over the years ahead.

Staff

The dedicated efforts of DIT's staff members at all grades over many years have brought the Institute to its present stage of development. The further development of the Institute will be equally dependent on their commitment, knowledge, expertise, talent, imagination, goodwill and hard work in the years ahead.

The human resource policies of the Institute should be formulated to empower staff members to fulfil their responsibilities to their students, to the Institute and to society to the highest standard. While based fundamentally on the partnership principle, these policies must aim to help each staff member to continuously develop, retain and improve her/his professional expertise and participate actively in the development of the Institute and its facilities. They should seek to develop in staff members an in-depth and up-to-date knowledge of their disciplines and subjects. They should also develop a spirit of peer collaboration and teamwork, committed to achieving excellence in all aspects of the work of the Institute. They should especially facilitate the provision of education to the students, inspiring them with a thorough knowledge of their disciplines, the capacity to continue to learn and develop personally throughout their careers.

These ideas should underpin the general approach to recruitment, induction, allocation, training, development, welfare and encouragement, as well as to job specifications in relation to all grades of staff — academic, administrative, library and technical support, maintenance and reception, porters and security.

External strategic relationships and collaborations

In addition to the successful partnership with the University of Dublin that has been in operation for over twenty-five years, and is now developing in new directions, the Institute should value academic collaboration and co-operation with other third level institutions in this country, as well as internationally. Proposals for joint courses or for the DIT's involvement in or validation of courses conducted elsewhere, or for other forms of co-operation, should continue to be welcomed and responded to positively, recognising that the DIT has much to benefit from and contribute to such initiatives.

The DIT is an active participant in a wide range of EU programmes involving student and staff exchange with universities and other third level institutions across Europe. The Institute should continue to recognise the importance of these links, seeking their further development, expansion and integration into the work of the Institute. Accordingly the DIT should commit itself to providing the organisational and administrative support to facilitate and encourage staff and students to enter into these exchanges and avail of the educational benefits and personal development that can result from them.

Links between the Institute and industry/commerce include:

- research and development and consultancy co-operation
- using professionals as external examiners for courses and as members of course and programme advisory boards
- provision of opportunities for student work placements as an integral part of many courses
- obtaining feedback from tens of thousands of DIT graduates in employment on courses and other programmes of the Institute.

These links provide considerable peer review to help to ensure the continuing currency of the DIT's syllabuses and courses. The Institute's policy is to continue to develop and strengthen these industrial relationships through mechanisms such as course and faculty advisory or liaison boards in different areas. It is envisaged that, where appropriate, it will be possible to include a period of industrial or commercial work placement or international placement as an integral part of more undergraduate courses.

The Institute has long-standing links with local government agencies such as County Councils and Corporations, as well as with state agencies such as Enterprise Ireland, FÁS, CERT and others. It should be Institute policy to continue to positively develop and build these collaborative links.

The colleges which now constitute the DIT have for over a hundred years had close links with a wide range of professional bodies, preparing students for membership examinations and providing further education and training opportunities for their members. It should be the policy of the Institute to continue to develop these relationships. In this way some of the professional bodies may be freed from the direct tasks of syllabus design and examinations. The Institute can provide academic elements, with an emphasis on quality assurance to appropriate academic standards. The professional bodies will make key inputs to course committees by way of advice and feedback, and by providing members for validation and review panels and to act as external examiners.

It has long been recognised that the numbers of students entering third level education from Dublin and the surrounding region are substantially lower than from the rest of the country. Entry rates from the more disadvantaged areas in Dublin are very low. The DIT policy to develop effective access mechanisms and link programmes to address this situation will be given high priority. There are formal links with a number of second level City of Dublin Vocational Education Committee (CDVEC) schools which facilitate the offering of places on a limited selection of courses to applicants from Post-Leaving Certificate courses and the policy will be to develop and expand these links. Within the DIT's open access policy, it is proposed to evaluate and implement, where appropriate, other mechanisms to develop these links, including outreach campaigns to schools and neighbourhoods, open days in the DIT schools, reserving numbers of places on specific courses, introducing more foundation and transition courses, as well as scholarships and special tutoring arrangements. Such arrangements are currently under active development by the Institute in collaboration with external organisations, such as the Dublin Chamber of Commerce.

The location of the different colleges of the Institute at the centre of the city of Dublin must be taken as an opportunity to put down roots deep in the local community. In the immediate hinterland of each college there are ranges of businesses, areas for development and considerable population numbers. Each such hinterland can offer a variety of modalities in which the local college or the Institute as a whole can develop the services it offers and allow the Institute to provide help and even leadership in local community development. The Institute must investigate the feasibility of a proactive policy of forming local coalitions for development.

A learning organisation

Modern applied technical knowledge and knowledge technologies, together with critical reflection on them, must be at the core of the DIT's values and activities. Internally, it must focus clearly on learning, developing and correcting courses, improving, enhancing and growing more flexibility and trust, listening, responding and interacting constructively with the outside world, and in general, becoming an intellectual powerhouse and a learning organisation in this technological age.

STUDENTS IN THE INSTITUTE

The Institute has a positive record of giving personal attention to its students. In delivering a personalised higher education service, the DIT will continue to place the education and professional development of the student as a person in the broadest sense at the centre of the Institute's values and agenda. This will enable the Institute's graduates to continue to contribute effectively to providing industrial, commercial and social leadership in Irish and European society.

The Institute's policy over the next five years will be that all its courses, including its assessment and examination arrangements, will be modularised. Credit accumulation will be introduced and this will provide very flexible programmes for the widest range of students. This will be linked to the introduction of a system of assessment and accreditation of prior learning. Students will be facilitated to pursue courses in a wide range of modes — full-time, extended part-time, block release and others. It will also help students who wish to take part-time work, or even full-time work, for periods during their courses. When fully implemented this measure will remove the distinction between full-time and part-time courses and will enable classes to be timetabled throughout the day from 8.00 am to 10.00 pm.

The Institute is committed to developing policies to attract and cater for a greater number of mature students in all its programmes.

It is Institute policy to provide a student handbook for each course or programme offered. The salient features of such a handbook are set out in the Course Quality Assurance Handbook. In general the student handbook provides information and guidance to the student on course syllabuses, timetables, class schedules, examination arrangements, and other details about the student's course and the Institute, its facilities and services.

A key feature and characteristic of the Institute which will continue is the ladders of educational opportunities which enable students to transfer vertically or horizontally to fulfill their career aspirations as effectively as possible within the Institute or through other higher education institutions in Ireland or elsewhere in Europe.

Work is currently underway in the Academic Council to analyse student completion rates. This issue will be addressed by the Teaching and Learning Resource Centre on an Institute-wide basis in order to improve retention rates, especially in first years of courses. Student examination performance will be correlated with original selection criteria and efforts will be made to retain students until they have achieved an appropriate level of academic award.

The feasibility of alternative modes of course delivery — distance learning, summer modules, the provision of foundation or linking modules for students entering higher level courses — will be examined. Such measures may involve using guest lecturers from outside the Institute. These can have the benefit of extending the use of the Institute buildings and facilities over a long working year.

In relation to each course, the staff/student meetings and student survey feedback about the course and its delivery are important means of improving learning opportunities and teacher/student relations, as is consulting with students about the programme and facilities provided. In this way the priorities and needs of the students can be identified. The feedback from the students is considered by the Course Committee, which recommends how issues arising might be addressed. Student membership is a key aspect of all committees in the Institute, including Course Committees.

A Student Charter of Rights is in preparation. It will spell out the facilities available, the rights of all students and students' responsibility for their own learning.

The Institute currently offers a very limited range of facilities to students but it is committed to greatly improving and expanding these, including recreational and sporting facilities. It is Institute policy to provide a range of playing fields and covered sports facilities, gymnasia and halls.

The Institute's policy is to improve the welfare, counselling and assistance services for students and it is the priority, in general, to continue to be a caring organisation.

A PROUD HISTORY, A FUTURE OF PROMISE

The DIT will continue to be a vital national educational asset in the heart of Dublin.

With a "long and distinguished record of advancing knowledge and promoting learning, particularly in their industrial and social applications", the Institute plays a "unique role in higher education in Ireland".

The DIT will continue to be oriented towards the community, the economy and the client with a strong emphasis on service and applied knowledge, opening up avenues for part-time study, for "non-traditional" students and providing opportunities for individuals to broaden their practical knowledge and competence by combining the academic and applied approaches to learning.

The strategic plan will set out the methods by which the DIT, as a multi-level, multi-function institution, will maintain its history of success and achievement and transform itself successfully to meet the new conditions and new challenges of the new century.

Index